Massacre at Alamein?

Were Generals Wavell and Auchinleck treated unjustly and was Montgomery over-rated during the desert wars of 1940/41, 1941/42 and 1942/43?

BOB LEACH

بوب ليتش

RAF 'Intelligence', GHQ, Cairo,
Navigator, Rawnsleys's Desert Patrol,
Attached South African Survey,

Wavell's War, 1940/41
Auchinleck's War, 1941/42
Montgomery's War 1942/43

A Square One Publication

A typical set of Review notices on a Bob Leach book

Marguerite Wolff, Adventures of a Concert Pianist
by Robert Clarson-Leach

Book Reviews and Appraisals

BOOK OF THE WEEK, Yorkshire Evening Post. 'Marguerite grew up to play in jails and jungle locations as well as the world's greatest halls and salons and embassies of Europe.'

Jim Greenfield

'The YEP's review is fabulous – congratulations.'
Vivian Stuart, Author, **The Australians**, (USA sales over 5 million).

'It is a unique story . . . the moments of tragedy that have shadows Miss Wolff's life (thankfully outnumbered by more happy events) are revealed with admirable candour . . . and with the stamp of unassailable authority which informs the fluently-written pages of this intriguing volume.'

Robert Mattew-Walker, Editor, **Music and Musicians**

'Here she tells of her passion for music and the story of her comeback (following the death of her husband) . . . She has received the additional accolade of having her biography published, written by Robert Clarson-Leach.'

Sally Brompton, **The Times**

'The first thing to say is how enthrallingly written it is . . . she could not have found a better biographer.'

Keith Fagan, **The Liszi Society**.

'She lives in an elegant London home in Belgravia with three Steinway pianos dotted around the house.'

Shirley Davenport, **Evening Gazette**.

'She wears a new Hartnell dress for the launching of her biography,'

Nigel Dempster, **The Daily Mail**.

'Marguerite Wolff might be described as accident prone . . . a chance meeting in prison led to her biography . . . the book jacket picture was taken, naturally, by Snowdon.'

Chronicler. **The Jewish Chronicle**

'A wonderfully gossipy chapter on clothes . . . the book comes surprisingly up to date with the Dikko affair and Mrs Ghandi's assassination.'

Leonard Pearcey, **Classical Music**.

'Piano playing can lead to some strange situations.'

Shirley Davenport, **The Yorkshire Post**.

'She turned to Solomon for a wider view of music . . . she found that Kentner's tuition was exhilarating. Marguerite's story is full of the expected chatter of the artist's room in concert halls around the world. Always slim and elegant she has many admirers in music, art and diplomacy.'

E. Alan Smith, **The Daily Telegraph**.

'There's many a so-called "best-selling" author who would like to have reviews like these!'

Diane Pearson, Author, **Csardas**, etc.

'I congratulate you on the prodigious impact which the book has made on the public, and not only on the musical world: that is a triumph these days.'

Charles Cleall, **Composer**.

'What a charming present!'

The Lady Diana Cooper.

By the same author

The Robert Clarsons, as writers, go back to 1855 when the author's great uncle Robert Clarson founded the *Macclesfield and Congleton Mercury*. The second Robert Clarson took over the running of the paper well into the 20th century. Robert Clarson-Leach entered journalism and writing in the late 1930's and now, in his 70s is still active. His son, christened Robert Clarson Leach, writes under the name of Robert Leach and has had over 20 books published (Legal, Law, Business, Taxation) since the 1960s.

Bob Leach has written most of his books under the name Robert Clarson-Leach, and these books, usually commissioned, include:

BERLIOZ, His Life and Times	Midas Books, then Artmusique, and Baton Press, and later in paperback by Music Sales, ISBN 0 7119 0829 X
In America	HIPPOCRENE BOOKS INC., New York
MARGUERITTE WOLFF, Adventures of a Concert Pianist.	(Book of the Week, Yorkshire Post).
MOZART AND HIS MAGIC FLUTE CLOCK	(Mechanical Music).
THE ART OF SPELLING	
THE ART OF LETTER WRITING	
COAL, NATURAL GAS,	(Educational books... Mullers)
HOW THE PLANETS RULE THE SUPERSTARS...	pub, Everest Books.
MECHANICAL MUSIC AND THE GREAT COMPOSERS.	Midas and MBSGB.
DEBUSSY.	Baton Press
BOB LEACH YEAR BOOK FOR 1984	
ASTROLOGY AND CLASSICAL MUSIC	
SELF PUBLISHING AND DIY PROMOTION	
VERGIE DERMAN, DANCING WITH THE ROYAL BALLET.	(Hardback & Paperback)

Editor... The Music Box

Radio plays, including:
DAVID SOMETHING (Charles Dickens with Emily Bronte)
THE MIDNIGHT MONSTER
LITTLE KOHAR

Bob Leach is a member of the Chartered Institute of Journalists.

He was also Head of English for a time at one of the largest schools in UK, 2000 pupils and a Department of 23 teachers of English (Garratt Green, Wandsworth, London.)

Limited First Paperback Edition 1996 by
Square One Publications,
The Tudor House
Upton upon Severn, Worcs. WR8 0HT

© Bob Leach (who also writes as Robert Clarson-Leach) 1996

All rights, World and National, remain with the author and are available for publishers worldwide who might wish to publish a second edition. All rights herewith reserved. No part may be stored on a retrieval system, or transmitted in any form, or by any means, electronic, mechanical, photocopying, or otherwise. Reviewers however, should they wish, are free to quote passages in connection with a review for inclusion in a newspaper, magazine, radio or TV broadcast. Readers with strong opinions FOR or AGAINST those expressed in this book are invited to put such opinions in writing to the author, c/o Square One Publications, Upton upon Severn.

British Library Cataloguing in Publication Data

Leach, Bob
   Massacre At Alamein?
   I. Title
   823.914 [F]

ISBN 1 899955 09 7

Copyright permission for use of photographs has in all cases been applied for and have been used in good faith. Any inadvertent misuse of copyright will be rectified by formal application once it is brought to the notice of the author.

Typeset in 10pt Times by Avon Dataset Ltd, The Studio, Waterloo Road, Bidford-on-Avon, B50 4JH
Printed by Antony Rowe, Chippenham

Dedicated to

Flt/Lt Derek Rawnsley, RAFVR,
and his wife
Flt/Officer Brenda Rawnsley, WAAF, M.E.,
and the men of
Derek Rawnsley's 'Long Range
Intelligence' (LRI) Desert Patrol,
October 1941 to November 1942

Derek Rawnsley was killed on
Flying duties, Middle East
22 February 1943.

Introduction

On Saturday May 6th 1995 my old Survey friend Phil Lambert, the artist, and three friends were driven from Southampton to The Albert pub in Victoria, London, for the annual reunion of the 512 R.E. Survey Company which served in the Middle East from January 1940 to 1945. In the rear window of the car Lambert had placed a placard, FOUR DESERT RATS FROM WAVELL'S 30,000! (Actually it was nearer 35,000. With this army Wavell defeated the 150,000 of Graziani's Italian Army, a feat described by one Military Historian as being 'unparalleled in British Military History'.)

1992 saw the 50th anniversary of The Battle of Alamein, and the tributes to Montgomery flew in.

1995 saw the 50th anniversary of the end of the war in Europe, and the tributes to Montgomery flew in.

Maybe as far as Europe is concerned the tributes are justified. I do not know.

What I do know it that the tributes reference the Desert Battles are not justified. At times my blood boils at the way Wavell, Auchinleck and Gott are dismissed as irrelevant and all the credit is heaped on to Montgomery.

If I say Alamein was a Massacre and Montgomery a Monster am I being rational and fair? In this book I present my case, having experienced the following:

... witnessed Wavell's 1940/41 battle from strips of Air Survey photos while serving at RAF Intelligence, GHQ, Cairo

... witnessed Auchinleck's 1941/42 battle while serving as a navigator in Derek Rawnsley's RAF Intelligence Desert Patrol. (LRDG),

... witnessed Montgomery's 1942/43 battle from Air Survey photos while attached to the South African Survey Unit based at Maadi (Cairo) mapping the progress of the battle and drawing target maps.

Thus I gained comprehensive knowledge of the three desert campaigns, and I lived in Cairo for five years and heard military and civilian opinions. The desert wars were my military life and I feel that I know and understand them.

My book poses these questions: *Were Generals Wavell and Auchinleck treated unjustly and did Montgomery, by deliberately jettisoning Auchinleck's 1942 blueprint for victory at the Alamein, needlessly lose thousands of lives?*

Read and judge for yourself.

© Bob Leach, East Sussex, 1995

Contents

ONE	All Quiet on the Western (Desert) Front	1
TWO	Mussolini Declares War. Life in Cairo.	5
THREE	In the Desert With Wavell	11
FOUR	In the Desert With Auchinleck	20
FIVE	The Secret of Alamein	30
SIX	The Censored *Asthenia of Rommel	40
SEVEN	How 'Private Armies' were Formed.	50
EIGHT	GOTT STRAFFE ROMMEL.	69
NINE	Churchill's Desert Dilemma.	79
TEN	Montgomery in Egypt	93
ELEVEN	Montgomery's Folly at Alamein. How the Battle should have been fought	109
TWELVE	Let us now Praise Famous Men	163

* Asthenia: Loss of Strength

Illustrations and Maps

Desert Patrol	viii
The Alamein Canal Project	32
Derek Rawnsley's Desert Patrol	68
512 R.E. Survey Detachment	78
General von Thoma surrenders to Montgomery	149
Map One	153
Map Two	156
Map Three	158
At the Going Down of the Sun	166

Derek Rawnsley's RAF Desert Patrol, 'Part of the LRDG'.

from THE VOICE OF WAR, edited by Victor Selwyn, published by Michael Joseph Ltd. (the Penguin Group Ltd.) 1995 . . . (p19, The Middle East, 1940–42) . . . *'enjoyed a freedom for which is known no parallel, a paradise for the independent and eccentric. The Army wrote its own rule book.' . . .', (Cairo) . . . became the cultural centre of war outside Britain'*, and . . . *'A character named Popski ran a private army whilst the Long Range Desert Group roamed behind enemy lines.'*

Another such patrol was that of Derek Rawnsley, RAFVR. By coincidence the respective navigators of these two patrols, Alec Petrie and Bob Leach, not only came from the Royal Engineers Survey but they began their prewar survey career on the same day . . . at Lamberhurst, Kent, 1937, working for The Ordnance Survey.

CHAPTER ONE

All Quiet on the Western (Desert) Front.

There were loyal mutterings of 'unjust treatment' by some old stagers at GHQ Cairo when Wavell was sacked in June 1941. The implied excuse from far-off Whitehall was 'failure in the desert', or thoughts to that effect. It was so unjust, this unquestioned placing of blame. After all, the decision to withdraw troops from the desert and send them to Greece had been Churchill's. If anyone ought to have been sacked it should have been Anthony Eden. He had been sent to Cairo and Athens to review the situation and it was he who recommended help for Greece.

Wavell, with a mere 36,000 men had captured 150,000 Italians in Libya between 12th December 1940 and the end of January 1941 and had advanced 500 miles and taken the ports of Derna and Tobruk and occupied the capital city, Benghazi. A stroke of military genius if ever there was one.

The Wavell momentum in January 1941 could probably have cleared the occupying Italians right along the North African coast as far as Tripoli and thus out of Libya altogether. This would have been long before Rommel was ready to perform his act of rescue in March and April.

It was when Wavell was on the point of complete victory that a German advance towards Greece, via the Balkans, seemed likely and Churchill pondered over whether to transfer some of Wavell's troops to Greece or to let the desert war race on to completely clear North Africa of the Italian Army.

Britain had a pact with Athens to defend Greece if Hitler attacked, but this defence could only be supplied if men were available. The problem was, should Britain go for complete victory in the desert or should the desert forces be weakened to help Greece? There is little doubt that Wavell and his famous 'Desert Rats' were for one overall victory in North Africa rather than risk two defeats, one in North Africa and one in Greece. As it happened, history shows that Churchill's decision to weaken Wavell only produced the two defeats: Libya and Greece.

If Wavell had been left to his own devices and had swept the desert clear of the Italian Fascists there may well have been no need for further desert battles, under Auchinleck in 1941/42, and for Churchill's directive to Field Marshall Alexander in June 1942 to '*destroy as soon as possible the (Axis) Army in North Africa . . . !*' If only that 1942 directive had been sent to Wavell in January 1941. It could have saved those men who died during Auchinleck's command 1941/42 and also it would have prevented the terrible loss of life under Montgomery 1942/43, especially in the actual Battle of Alamein on October 23rd 1942.

This, of course, is written with the advantage of hindsight. The main reason for writing this book is to set the record straight on behalf of the reputations of the sacked Generals Wavell and Auchinleck who were unfairly removed from command and undeservedly humiliated.

Anthony Eden was not the best person to judge Middle East conditions and history confirms this because in July 1956 when Nasser seized the Suez Canal the actions of Prime Minister Eden were immediately condemned by America and the United Nations. Eden became ill from the worry of it all (in November 1956 he flew to Jamaica for 'a rest'). Britain agreed to withdraw from Egypt, the Suez Canal problem was handed to the United Nations to settle with Nasser, and in January 1957 Eden resigned and Macmillan became Prime Minister. So much for Eden's ability to fathom the peculiar mysteries of the Middle East!

To support the contention that General Wavell received less than his just deserts let us first examine the military facts and political implications germane to the rise and fall in Egypt of General Sir Archibald Wavell.

In 1940 Wavell had only the Italians to contend with in North Africa. Hitler had no ambition for German participation in a war south of the

Mediterranean Sea. The German leader was content to keep the war away from the Middle East.

British troops were in Egypt to 'protect' such important interests as the Suez Canal, military bases in the Middle East, Alexandria harbour, events in Palestine to the north and Sudan in the south, and also to keep any Arab pro-Nazi sympathies under control. The British Ambassador in Cairo, Sir Miles Lampson, kept a watchful eye on the Egyptian Government and an arrogantly patronising eye on the Boy King, Farouk, who had a strong liking for Italy and an easily understood hatred of British domination in his country, Egypt.

The French, too, were keen to avoid military conflict in the Middle East.

In short, Germany and France were fully occupied concentrating on the European battlefield and would, at that stage, have played no part in preventing Wavell removing the Italians from Libya.

The British had not wished to be the first to make a move against the Italians. So long as the Italians stayed their side of 'the Wire' (the fence erected on Mussolini's orders to separate Cyrenaica, Libya's eastern territory, from Egypt) the Anglo-Egyptian forces on their side would 'stay put'.

The Italian people themselves had little heart to fight the British who, after all, had been their ally in the First World War. It was the Italian dictator, Mussolini, acting as an opportunist, who believed that he saw a chance to enlarge his Empire in Africa by invading Egypt. The Italian dictator, anxious to travel on the back of Hitler's 1938 to 1940 successes, also thought that this was a time to claim the Mediterranean Sea for Italy and thus control the Suez Canal.

On June 10th 1940 Mussolini declared war on Britain.

This was the catalyst for military activity on the border between Egypt and Cyrenaica and for Italy to bomb Gibraltar, Alexandria, Malta, and other targets including British shipping in the Mediterranean, a sea which Mussolini now boasted of as 'Mare Nostrum'.

It was, therefore, Mussolini who instigated war in the Western Desert.

The desert fighting was quite unique, considered by many to be rather sporting (neither side ever poisoned the water holes during the backward and forward surges of the campaign). There were no towns, factories, or civilians to get in the way of the 'War Games'. (In November 1941 the captured German General von Ravenstein, reflecting on the desert war up until then, declared it to be a 'gentleman's war'.)

There were to be three annual battles, rather like three football seasons each beginning in autumn of one year and closing down for the summer of the next year, viz; 1940/41 season, General Wavell, 1941/42, General Auchinleck, and 1942/43 season, General Montgomery.

The pitch was the open desert.

There was only one road and that followed the coastline, as did the single rail track from Alexandria to Mersa Matruh. The only buildings were the colonisation houses which Mussolini had built along the coast from Derna to Benghazi and buildings at coastline towns such as Mersa Matruh.

The Egyptian forces of the Anglo-Egyptian Defence were removed from 'the Wire' and Battle Headquarters was set up at Baggush, with some forward troops at Mersa Matruh.

The troops sat and waited.

CHAPTER TWO

Mussolini Declares War. Life in Cairo.

Major-General R.N. O'Connor (Field Commander under General Wavell who had become Commander-in-Chief Middle East Command in August 1939) was called to take command of forces in the desert and he established Battle HQ at Maaten Baggush, about five miles east of Mersa Matruh.

O'Connor was an ironic choice to fight the Italians because he had fought alongside them in World War One. Now he commanded the 7th Armoured Division and his professional men became imbued with the romantic nomadic spirit of the desert and became known as The Desert Rats after the tiny desert creature, the jerboa.

The 7th Armoured Division occupied the forward position and behind them was the excellent 4th Indian Division.

The RAF, 202 Group, offered what help it could to General O'Connor with its Lysanders for reconnaissance and Blenheims and Gladiators for bombing raids on the Italian-held territory.

Nothing, perhaps, typifies the 'gentlemanly conduct' of 1940/41 desert warfare more than the note Sir Arthur Longmore (Commander-in-Chief Middle East Air Forces) sent to the Italians expressing sincere regret when Marshal Balbo was accidentally shot down by his own Italian Ack-Ack. Longmore's note was graciously acknowledged by the Italians.

An example of a general lack of enthusiasm for war by the Italians can be seen from early naval activity in the Mediterranean. The British

MASSACRE AT ALAMEIN?

Mediterranean Fleet put to sea one day after Mussolini declared war. The Fleet deliberately patrolled the waters the Italians would need to use if they wished to support their Army in Cyrenaica. Throughout June there was no response by the Italian Navy. Admiral Sir Andrew Cunningham thus established moral supremacy over the Italian Navy.

On November 11th 1940 the British Navy destroyed five battleships in Taranto harbour. Three were sunk and two were unfit to sail. This had a greatly beneficial effect on British morale. Things had been going badly for the Allies in Europe.

Cunningham knew, however, that if, or when, the Italians became more resolute the British would be in some difficulty because the Royal Navy was based at either end of the Mediterranean Sea (Gibraltar and Alexandria) with the Italians in the strong central position. (Eventually the British lost control of these waters and supplies for the Middle East arrived via the long journey round South Africa).

It was on 15th July 1940 that Mussolini ordered an Italian invasion of Egypt. Marshal Graziani, being in the desert and knowing of the lethal dangers of activity during the summer heat, protested. Mussolini, from the temperate climate of Rome, lost patience with his desert commander and so ordered an attack across 'the Wire' for 9th September. Graziani had no option but to advance into Egypt. The frontier town of Sollum fell first, then Halfaya Pass, and then the objective of the offensive, Sidi Barrani, fell to the Italians on September 16th. One could almost hear Mussolini boasting, 'I told you so!'

A halt was called by Graziani in order to prepare for the next objective, Mersa Matruh. Here the forward Allied troops were dug in, and waiting. The heat in the desert was terrific and Graziani refused to consider any further advance 'until November at the earliest', despite Mussolini's impatience. The marshal was aware that during his advance he had not come up against the full strength of the Allied Forces. Graziani was also aware that the further east he progressed the longer his supply lines would be. For example, about 100 miles of pipeline had to be laid to supply drinking water.

Throughout this narrative of war in the desert it will be seen that Mussolini in Rome, Churchill in London, and (later) Hitler in Berlin, had little understanding of desert warfare and the directives to their respective desert commanders were ill-advised on several occasions. This narrative will also attempt to show how and why those involved in war in Europe began to differ psychologically from those involved purely in war in the Egyptian Desert. People are, naturally, conditioned by events and environment and the events and environment in London and Cairo could not have been more opposite in character.

How could a Cairo-based serviceman write with clear conscience to, say, his girl friend and tell her of a fascinating evening at Shepheards Hotel when she has written to tell him that her office in London has been bombed and she has been evacuated to Berkhamstead, or tell his mother of a most charming visit to a late-night Garden Cinema when she has written telling him of an air raid on Liverpool and she as a Red Cross nurse has consequently been digging dead bodies out of bombed buildings.

Surely this great difference in wartime background was having an effect because there seemed to be little appreciation at the War Office in London for Wavell's strategic insight and his skilful handling of minimal forces when the desert campaign began in December 1940.

People in Britain had been traumatised by the terrible events of that year; Hitler gaining more and more territory in Europe with the fall of Denmark, Norway, Belgium, Holland, Paris and half of France, Dunkirk, the Battle of Britain, blackout, rationing, theatres closed, constant air raid warnings, nightly bombing and consequent death role, 'Britain Fights Alone!' and Churchill's famous speech reference the wonderful air crews of the RAF... *Never in the field of human conflict was so much owed by so many to so few.*

Those 'at home' suffered the terrible Blitz delivered by the German Luftwaffe. There was the devastation of Coventry, and Churchill wooing Roosevelt for help, and the people in Britain united as a solid team as never before. It was their greatest period in history. Their behaviour was superb.

These months of strife and deprivation understandably affected the viewpoint of the people living in the affected parts of war-torn Europe during 1940.

Contrast that awful background with that of people in Egypt during 1940.

MASSACRE AT ALAMEIN?

The troops already in Egypt in September 1939 plus those who joined them up to, say, the Spring of 1940 found themselves enjoying the luxury of what was to be Egypt's *belle epoque.*

Allied servicemen were invited into a social class the extravagance of which they had only witnessed in lavish Hollywood movies. The contrast with war-torn Europe could not have been more marked.

There was little concern in Egypt itself over the outcome of the desert war. Socially the atmosphere was relaxed. Shops displaying a Union Jack outside had an Italian flag under the counter. An occupying army was good for business. It made up for the absent tourist trade.

On arriving in Cairo in the 1930s or early 1940, whether it be to GHQ Cairo, Abbassia Barracks, The Citadel (barracks), Qasr el Nil Barracks, or a private hotel, one was immediately transported mentally and physically into an Oriental Paradise. As long ago as the 14th century the travel writer Ibn Battuta described Cairo as a mother of cities and seat of the Pharaohs . . . *peerless in beauty and splendour.* That is how I saw it in January 1940.

At the end of the 19th century Ishmail built the familiar area of new Cairo (old Cairo became a derelict area, abandoned by superstitious fellahin who might otherwise have inhabited it . . . as indeed they do now at the end of the 20th century, their fears assuaged by the need for space to accommodate the ever-increasing population) between the banks of the Nile and what had been the Ezbekiya swampland but now housed the famous Cairo Opera House, Shepheards Hotel, Opera Square, the Grand Continental, Ezbekiya Gardens (named after the Egyptian hero Emir Ezbek), and the glorious shopping streets; Sharia Soliman Pasha, Qasr el Nil, and Emad el Din. Glamorous Garden Cinemas flourished late into the night showing American and Continental films with sub-titles in Arabic, English, as required. The new Metro cinema with its sliding roof equalled in grandeur the cinemas in London and Paris. The 'English' bookshop was better stocked than it could have been in London, having on display banned books such as *Lady Chatterley's Lover*, and gently illustrated pornography. Famous night clubs such as The Auberge du Pyramides (one of King Farouk's favourites), on the Mena Road out to the Pyramids at Giza, welcomed visitors, and Mena House Hotel allowed troops to use its outdoor swimming pool.

MASSACRE AT ALAMEIN?

Famous clubs such as Gezira Sporting Club, the Turf Club, Maadi Sporting Club, and so on, opened their doors to 'honorary members', and prominent citizens 'did their bit for the war' by opening their homes to selected members of the Allied Forces.

Saturation point in hospitality did not happen until later in 1940, at which point Cairo Society closed ranks with those lucky ones it had already enrolled, unless a new arrival happened to be 'a star' or a millionaire or extremely handsome.

The layout of this modern area of Cairo reminds one of Paris. The hotels, however, were described as 'English managed' and the city itself as 'the Englishman's playground'.

The British in Egypt during the first half of the 20th century benefited from the social ascendency gained during Kitchener's time when the 'English way of living' was the standard accepted by upper class Cairenes. Almost everyone of any standing could speak English, French and Arabic, and many could speak Turkish, Hebrew and other languages too.

Princess Nazli, who was to become Queen of Egypt, was notoriously snobbish in her 'English' ways. Private teachers and nannies were invariably English.

Society cafes became the equivalent of the gentlemen's clubs in London's Pall Mall and one's position in Egyptian Society determined which cafe (club) one was accepted in, and these centres became pivots of British rule in Egypt.

The British found 'life's pleasures' cheap and plentiful.

Horse racing at Gezira Sporting Club rivalled in splendour that at Epsom or Ascot.

Thus was the fashion set for champagne lunch parties with young men in straw boaters and elegant young ladies in white cotton dresses enjoying foie gras sandwiches, cold beer served by uniformed (usually Nubian) servants, and sitting on wicker chairs set on lush lawns under attractive palm trees. That was Gezira Club. That was the style. That was what welcomed the British arrivals in 1939 and early 1940.

How could the British in England and the British in Cairo have the same view of war? or think the same? or even behave the same?

Two events did cause a stutter in the high jinks of fun-loving Cairo; first the Fall of Paris in June, and second in July when Mussolini entered the Egyptian desert.

Still, Sidi Barrani was 400 miles from Cairo. Plenty of warning as to which flag to fly outside the shop!

June and July only caused a slight falter in step. High Society closed ranks and continued to enjoy life to its luxurious full. Once the two shocks had subsided life in the fleshpots of Egypt and in the Garden City of The Upper Classes continued in sybaritic luxury. People 'back home' might well have asked, don't these people know there's a war on?

(The Egyptians could have replied, of course, "Well, it isn't *our* war!"

CHAPTER THREE

In the Desert, with Wavell.

Chapter Two paints a rosy picture of life in Cairo.

Chapter Three shows the other side of the penny.

Alas, now, for newly-arrived Allied Forces entering the Middle East. No journey by rail across France followed by a pleasant Mediterranean cruise. Mussolini had acted. Allied shipping to the Middle East had an eight or ten week Atlantic voyage, threatened by German U boats, and then sailing round the Cape and up the sweltering Indian Ocean to the Red Sea and Suez. All these troops saw of Cairo was during the time of a 48-hour pass.

Take nurse Betty Parkin, early 1941, ('Desert Nurse', published by Robert Hale). After a quick 'shufti' at Cairo and a number 14 tram to the Pyramids it was off to the Canal Zone. Damned mosquitoes. A few months later these vicious biting insects brought Betty low with malaria. She writes that the toilets at the makeshift hospital were wooden seats over buckets. Sand, too, was a curse. It covered everything and got into one's shoes, underclothing, neck, eyes . . . And of the murderous sandstorms Betty writes, '*gentle women turned into shrill-voiced vixens*'.

Squadron-Leader G.W. Houghton in his book, '*They Flew Through Sand*' (first published in Cairo) begins, '*We were probably the most miserable airmen in the world. The sky was the colour of an old penny, and a tornado, like the hot wind from a hairdresser's drying machine, was sweeping up from the south. Visibility was nil. We were at Gambut* (near the border between Cyrenaica and Egypt. In 1940 O'Connor used it temporarily as his HQ, and for a time in 1941 Rommel used it as *his* HQ) *'where it is stormy about 350 days each year. In silence we suffered, desperately clinging to the torn canvas* (of the tent). *The storm lasted three hours.'*

Jake Wardrop, in his book, *'Tanks Across the Desert'*, writes of the desert in late 1940. *'We left for Mersa Matruh in a blinding sandstorm'*

Of Wavell's victory over Graziani, Wardrop reports how Sir Basil Liddell-Hart described Wavell's advance . . . *'It was one of the most daring ventures and breathless races in the annals of the British Army.'*

One can seriously doubt if London saw the desert war as now being described in this Chapter Three. The luxury described in Chapter Two is more likely to have been in the imagination of those in Britain. Perhaps this misunderstanding had something to do with Churchill's valuation of Wavell's efforts. The desert was not a vista of eroticly-curved creamy sand dunes lying warmly under a desert sun and a perpetually blue sky. *'War in the Desert'* by James Lucas gives a truer picture of the desert scene.

' *"The blue" was by common definition a right bastard. It might have been a paradise for tacticians, but it was a harsh and ruthless tyrant. It was a foretaste of Hell. There was little water, no restaurants, no bars, no cinemas, no comfort, no sex. Instead, there were flies, fleas, scorpions, and a few snakes.'*

The surface over which the fighting took place was grit, with a dirty grey-brown crust, the product of centuries of erosion of the limestone rock.

Flies settled on everything, and maggots appeared as if by magic to cover the open wounds of dead bodies. The surface was such that anything moving on it threw up dust. To drive behind another vehicle was to drive blindly into an ever-present cloud of choking dust, even if driving very slowly.

When it rained on the coastal strip of the desert vehicles became bogged down in a quagmire. At other times soft sand gripped men and vehicles and some have been known to sink beneath the lethal 'Sandy Sea'. Another handicap to progress was the sudden appearance of a wadi (dried-up valley) which was often difficult to cross and may have required a big detour.

Only the camel trains marched on regardless. The war in the desert had little effect on them. The desert Arabs would cheerfully barter with any *askari*, (soldier), whether he be British, Indian, Italian, German, ... completely disinterested in who might or might not be winning the war. Invading armies had been busy in Egypt for thousands of years.

Churchill, with the Italians pouring into the Egyptian Desert in July 1940, thought that he would like to have a look at and a chat with his desert commander so in August Wavell was summoned to London.

Although the British Prime Minister was impressed by much of what Wavell advocated and by the praise others had stated on the general's behalf Churchill was, nevertheless, not fully appreciative of Wavell's quiet almost philosophical demeanour. The general was not a talker gifted in inspiring listeners. Rather was he a doer gifted in inspiring followers. Churchill had doubts whether Wavell was the man to make best use of the very limited forces available in the desert. London had doubts. Cairo had no doubts. But then London and Cairo had become in outlook as different as chalk and cheese.

Churchill and Wavell did have intellectual similarities, especially in their extensive general knowledge and love of literature and poetry but Churchill was less likely to quote poetry to an unwary listener. The pictures in Churchill's mind he painted (physically) on canvas. The pictures in Wavell's mind were woven by words of poetry (i.e., in the mind). Wavell wrote, *'My As. O. C. have to listen when I quote verse to them ... that is the privilege of a Commander-in-Chief. My wife and daughter have quietly but firmly cured me of the habit as far as they are concerned,'* and with his wry sense of humour he continues, *'I would warn young men, when they find young women willing to listen to poetry, to watch their steps carefully'*. Wavell's collection of poetry was collected by his son and published as *'Other Men's Flowers'*. by Jonathan Cape. Churchill's only novel, *'Savrola'*, published originally by Longmans, is a youthful story (Churchill was 23) about an imaginary Ruritanian-type country, Laurania. Savrola is the hero, loved by his nanny rather than by his mother (home truths?) and Savrola's purpose in life is to save his people!

Although on different wavelengths Churchill and Wavell were a couple of dreamers destined not to see eye to eye.

MASSACRE AT ALAMEIN?

Wavell returned to Egypt and he and O'Connor planned how best to beat the Italians. They gave the operation a code name, **COMPASS**, and it was intended as an exploratory raid lasting about five days. The key to success was secrecy, speed and surprise. Secrecy was very difficult in Egypt because Egypt was not at war. It was a democratic country with its own king and freely elected Parliament and they had no intention of taking part in the fighting if it could be avoided. There were no restrictions on the public, such as notices proclaiming 'The Walls Have Ears!'. The very atmosphere of Cairo 'had ears' and latticed windows provided a thousand and one peepholes, so cafe gossip was rife as individuals claimed to have special secret information as to what was happening at a safe distance in the desert.

The plans were made carefully and were not rushed. The date set for Operation **COMPASS** was 9th December, 1940.

During October and November Mussolini and Churchill were fuming at the inactivity of their respective armies 'lazing on the desert's Mediterranean coastline'. It was Wavell who made the first move.

Wavell and O'Conner deceived enemy air survey by using convoys of dummy tanks (disguised lorries) and dummy gun emplacements. RAF 202 would be sent on bombing raids in one area to distract Italian attention while Allied troops were secretly moved. On occasions air raids were made to cover the sound of advancing tanks. The result of this activity was to give the Italians an exaggerated estimate of Allied strength. The Desert Rats had *not* been lazing!

On the 9th December when Wavell struck the Italian tank crews were unready for action so when the British Matilda tanks burst through Italian encampments panic reigned. Sidi Barrani fell to the British as the Italians fled. The *modus operandi* in the desert war was for the advancing army to encircle the retreating enemy and for those thus trapped their role was to surrender. This is how reports of desert battles spoke of thousands of prisoners and only hundreds of dead, as against European battles reporting thousands of dead and only hundreds of prisoners, In the first three days O'Conner captured 38,000 prisoners at a cost of only 624 killed, wounded, or missing.

(A unique aspect of desert warfare was the manner in which troops reported as 'missing' turned up at unexpected times and in unexpected places, having walked to safety in the most individual and remarkable manner. This is evidence of the 'Lawrence of Arabia' understanding of the desert which Wavell's forces assimilated. The RAF created a 'Late Arrivals Club', founded in the Western Desert, June 1941, and each member was allowed to wear 'the emblem of the Winged Boot' on the left breast of his flying suit. A Cairo metal-beater produced an intial order of 50 such medals, with the approval of the A.O., C-in-C RAF, M.E.).

The Italians woke up from the shock of Wavell's advance and General Bergonzoli, affectionately known as 'Electric Whiskers', promised Mussolini that Bardia would not fall. Bergonzoli had 40,000 men and 400 guns and ample stocks, and he truly felt assured that Bardia would not fall. Based on the numbers of men employed by each side it should not have fallen. But it did. The Desert Rats took Bardia on January 3rd 1941, with the capture of 40,000 prisoners, plus the 400 guns and the ample stocks. The assault was led by the Australians who suffered 456 casualties; killed, injured or missing.

Tobruk fell next to the Desert Rats (7th Armoured Div.) and another 25,000 prisoners were roped in, with about 400 casualties (k.i. or m.) to the 7th Armoured Division.

Before long the ports of Tobruk, Derna and Benghazi were ready to receive British shipping. On February 2nd 1941 a general withdrawal by Italians was in progress and Wavell looked set for total victory. A signal from London on February 13th informed Wavell that Greece was the priority and that an advance 'all the way' to Tripoli was ruled out.

That was the end of Operation **COMPASS.** The momentum was lost and, more significantly, Hitler became interested in North Africa. Rommel was sent and in March set about recapturing the territory Wavell had fought for and won from the Italians.

Whether it was right or wrong to halt Wavell to help the cause of the Greeks is debateable. What is sure, however, is that no blame can be laid at Wavell's door.

The Italian 10th Army had been annihilated.

So ended what could have been a glorious desert victory. Wavell's and O'Connor's tactics had been a model of imagination and boldness.

MASSACRE AT ALAMEIN?

At a cost of 500 killed the 36,000 Desert Rats had captured some 150,000 prisoners, over 800 guns of field gun size or larger, and more than 400 tanks. The Italian 5th Squadron Air Force had suffered such losses in the air and on the ground by the RAF Desert Air Force that this Italian squadron never again made a serious contibution to the Italian war effort.

General O'Connor returned to Cairo, the 7th Armoured Division was withdrawn to refit, the 6th Australian Division (no praise is too high for their contribution) was sent to Greece to be replaced in the desert by the inexperienced 9th Australian Division. The brilliant and experienced RAF 202 Desert Group was withdrawn to refit.

Wavell, unable to keep Benghazi, decided to retain his grip on the port of Tobruk. The Desert Rat spirit was such that the men marooned there by the German advance of Rommel's Afrika Korp maintained an agressive attitude rather than a defensive one. It was a brave ploy. The Tobruk force repeatedly went on sorties attacking the Germans and their supply lines, and the garrison (mainly Australian at the time) remained a constant thorn in Rommel's side because he was unable to capture this tiny port. An Australian band played every day in the main square.

Rommel had numerical superiority, fresh troops excited by German victories in Europe, and superior arms and ammunition. Wavell had depleted and tired forces and it was too much to ask them to do it all again.

But Churchill did.

Hence Operation **BATTLEAXE**.

Any neutral observer will surely admit that Wavell had little chance of winning this one.

Wavell retired to his former Battle HQ at Baggush, well into Egyptian territory. In May 1941 he had but 25,000 men. Churchill sent troops, tanks and equipment to Wavell, but they had to be transported via the long voyage round the Cape.

In order to occupy Rommel while plans for 'Battleaxe' were being made Wavell ordered Brigadier Strafer Gott to organize Operation **BREVITY** with the intention of driving the Germans from Sollum and Capuzzo. Gott, with two weak regiments of tanks and the 22nd Guards Brigade captured Halfaya Pass and Capuzzo and his cruisers drove on to Sidi Omar and pressed on to the ridge of Hafid. A German counter attack drove the Guards out of Capuzzo and pushed Gott and his forces back to Halfaya Pass and finally back to Baggush. The operation, although a failure, did show that in Brigadier Gott the British had yet another leader who understood the peculiarities of desert warfare, and one who was not afraid to attack superior (in number) forces and arms. Other men who were emerging included Colonel Jock Campbell and Brigadier Dorman-Smith. It augured well for the future of the war in the desert that British officers of this calibre were emerging.

Wavell's strategy was to bring Rommel to a standstill and in this he succeeded. Tobruk held firm and although Gott's operation had failed in May 1941 at least it had prevented Rommel from having the luxury of a lull during which he could have quietly made plans for the invasion of Egypt.

Air Marshall Tedder was now C-in-C M.E. Air Force and he worked well and successfully with General Wavell despite that fact that there were only 350 aircraft 'of all types' and an acute shortage of spares.

On June 14th, after many exhortations during May by Churchill for Wavell to begin the action, British columns quietly advanced towards 'the Wire'.

Operation **BATTLEAXE** had begun.

The 'Battleaxe' commander in the field was Lt.-General Sir Noel Beresford-Peirse. His forces included the 4th Indian Division under Major-General Frank Messervy, and the 7th Armoured Division under Major-General Sir Michael Creagh.

Rommel's intercept wireless service quickly alerted him to Wavell's advance. The Germans had the 15 Panzer Tank Division north of Capuzzo and the 5 Light Division near to the Tobruk environs. The minefields laid by the Germans and their powerful 88 mm guns halted the British tanks. Wavell's artillery could make little progress and failed in its objective, which was to take and control the Halfaya Pass.

The attack on Halfaya was one of a simultaneous three-pronged attack and the second, or central, drive was by the Guards Brigade and a regiment of Matilda tanks which reached Fort Capuzzo successfully but eventually had to retire against superior numbers.

The third prong, by the 7th Armoured Brigade, attacked the Hafid

Ridge suffering heavy losses, but some of the ground gained was held by the Desert Rats until they, too, had to retire.

The 'surprise' element of Wavell's victorious advance in 1940 was missing because Rommel could see the limited options open to Wavell and was able to remain one step ahead.

Also, it was the wrong time of the year to start a desert war. It was the end of the 1940/41 football season. Surely, the Desert Rats reasoned and thinking in sporting terms, it would be best to let the cricket season go by... to rebuild, train and prepare the new arrivals... and so be in readiness for the new 1941/42 season in, say, September or October. Rommel was held firm for the time being. But, Churchill had spoken, and the Desert Rats had to press on. The RAF reported that Rommel had vast numbers of troops streaming towards the battle area. It seemed to those involved pointless to struggle on in the merciless heat of the summer, with temperatures of up to 120 degrees.

After about four days of fighting Wavell had lost almost 1,000 men (k. w. or m.) and 91 tanks. There is no doubt that 'London' and 'Cairo' held vastly different views on how desert warfare should be handled.

Churchill, having sent equipment which included the new Mark IV Crusader tank to supplement the unpopular Matildas, did not seem to understand that there was an inevitable time lag between the arrival of the tanks at Suez and their readiness for desert action complete with trained crews. Tanks which could buzz quickly around Salisbury Plain were not nearly so mobile in the desert sand.

They needed, for example, sand-filters to be fitted, and alterations to the cooling systems. Tank commanders were worried about the mechanical efficiency under desert conditions, and the armour seemed much too thin to stand up to the German fire power, in particular the German 88 mm guns.

Even after overhaul at the workshops in the Egyptian Delta region a short drive of even 30 miles put 10% out of action. What percentage would it be in the real desert? Tank crews were reported as saying that they felt safer in an armoured 3-ton lorry because a German shell would merely blow a hole in the lorry, which would possibly still be able to drive on and which, more significantly, would not incinerate the crew as usually tragically happened when a Matilda or Crusader tank was hit.

On 21st June Wavell sent a cable to Churchill stating that the operation should not have been undertaken and, officer and gentleman, took the blame: I *was impressed by apparent need for immediate action,* and reported the failure of Operation Battleaxe.

Churchill, ignoring the fact that the pressure to advance had been his, decided that Wavell must go even though he had been beaten by superior numbers of forces and had, before that, been brilliant in victory until stopped by the needs of the Greek adventure. On June 21st Churchill sent a signal that Wavell must be replaced. The signal was read to Wavell as he was shaving, on June 22nd. He showed not the slightest emotion.

"The Prime Minister is quite right," he said. *"This job needs a new eye and a new hand."* And he went on shaving.

On July 5th 1941 General Sir Claude Auchinleck assumed command in Cairo.

GENERAL WAVELL

CHAPTER FOUR

In the Desert, with Auchinleck

General Auchinleck had already gained World War Two experience against the Germans, having led the expedition in Norway during April 1940 and having held on to Narvik until forced out in June when the British had to evacuate.

Churchill called Auchinleck to London in July 1941 but if the Prime Minister hoped to discover a 'Get-up-and-at-'em' man of impetuous action he was disappointed because his new desert commander turned out to be of the same mould as General Wavell; a man who would not rush into things, one who understood that living creatures in the desert need to move carefully and gently to survive. The British Prime Minister, on asking Auchinleck's opinion about immediate action against Rommel, was told that nothing must move until November, 1941. Churchill was not pleased about this and argued at great length but Auchinleck had the same patient demeanour as Wavell and for once Churchill felt helpless to impose his own will. (In fairness to Churchill we must remember that in the summer of 1941 he had more than enough on his plate and he was probably relieved to leave the desert problem in the hands of Auchinleck, at least for the time being.)

Auchinleck might not have won Churchill's heart but he won the delay he advocated and agreement was reached for a desert offensive to begin on November 1st, an operation which Auchinleck eventually named **CRUSADER.**

MASSACRE AT ALAMEIN?

A most valuable legacy which Auchinleck received from Wavell was the individually created 'Private Armies'. These desert patrols, often as small as six men sharing three armoured trucks, would drive southwards into the desert, then travel in a westerly direction until behind enemy lines. The patrol would then carefully move north and search for targets such as petrol dumps, supply depots, assembly points for aircraft, tanks or vehicles. The task for the patrol was to sneak in and fix time bombs. This was usually done during the night and once the demolition explosives had been set the patrol would disappear into the vast sandy-sea area of the southern sand dunes. A small group could thus inflict tremendous damage on the enemy. Air Survey frequently supplied patrols with map positions of suitable targets to attack.

The British had been leaders in the development of this type of desert-patrol activity whether it be for use in warfare or for civilian use in orthodox desert survey.

Major-General Eric Cole, whose first command was 4th Field Brigade, RA, Signal Section, in 1928, was posted to Signals at Abbassia Barracks in Egypt in 1929. He, with Royal Signals colleague Brigadier R.A. Bagnold, developed desert accessories such as the sun compass, water condenser, and the steel channels for moving vehicles trapped in soft sand and which proved essential to the exploits of the 1940s patrols of the Long Range Desert Group. Eric Cole's most important contribution to the efficiency of desert patrols was a wireless transmitter he first used in a 1500 mile desert expedition in 1934. Each night Cole was able to communicate with Signals at Abbassia (Cairo). Until 1934 such long-distance communication had been considered impossible but Eric Cole's successful experimentation led to each LRDG patrol having a 'wireless truck'.

A quiet and gifted man who shunned publicity Eric Cole was one of many sportsmen who loved the desert. He was Officers' Light Heavyweight boxing champion in 1928 but the following year, on leave from Egypt, he argued with the authorities that although he was an officer he could fight the legitimate finalist, who was 'other ranks', for the All Ranks Light Heavyweight title, which he won. He was also Army Golf champion and a fine billiards player. As a schoolboy, living in Dover, he financed his urge to experiment by claiming sixpence from car-owning neighbours who needed their car batteries charged. Eric's father wondered why the electricity bill was so high. Eric sought intellectual companionship in the Chelsea Arts Society. He was appointed CBE in 1945 and CB in 1960.

Brigadier R.A. Bagnold, who became Officer Commanding the LRDG, used Ford vans, 15cwt and 30 cwt, and became expert at fixing his position in the desert using theodolite, wireless, and the stars. He thus felt safe to discover routes previously considered unfit for motor transport and as his confidence grew he became unafraid of becoming bogged down in soft sand because he always managed to unload, dig, pull, lay planks, and finally devise the steel channels which solved the problem of sand-trapped vehicles.

Men in the LRDG were the most pleasant of people. Indeed, they had the same peaceful sense of comradely hospitality which was part and parcel of the Bedouin Arab's way of life. Like his friend, Eric Cole, Bagnold was a shy scholarly man. Wavell gave him complete freedom to pick the men he wanted, as did Auchinleck. Bagnold's favourite size for a patrol seemed to be one of five 30 cwt trucks with four or five men to a truck. A good friend of Bagnold's was Captain Bill Shaw, a veteran desert traveller who loved to go where he believed no man had trodden before. During the war Bill Shaw became an LRDG intelligence officer.

If you got lost in the desert? . . . Brigadier Bagnold's advice sums it all up.

"When you think you are lost in the desert, smoke a cigarette, take a short nap, and then start working out where you are."

Wavell, approached in 1940 by Bagnold, gave him every encouragement and the 'individual freedom of thought' which the desert seems to infiltrate into the psyche of the Empire troops (New Zealanders and Australians simply loved to serve in these patrols) made them an elite corps. The members dressed like bandits and were threatened with death by Josef Goebbels, if captured in the desert, because 'only soldiers properly dressed will be afforded the protection of the Geneva Convention governing Prisoners of War'.

The Germans feared these patrols and Wavell and Auchinleck allowed them the 'freedom of the desert', and thus was created the famous Long Range Desert Group.

David Stirling went one stage further, adding parachute jumping and attacks in theatres of war other than the desert. He created the even more famous SAS, Special Air Service, still effectively active to this day, with terrifying efficiency.

There must have been times when Rommel wondered what he was doing in the desert. Werner Haupt, in his book *North African Campaign* wrote: *The German command never appreciated the importance of the Mediterranean for the security of its supply lines. As a result the Afrika Korps was left on its own.*

The German Airforce was unable to subdue Malta so Rommel's supply ships could not be relied on to successfully reach Tripoli. It was more important to Hitler that the Luftwaffe hitherto in Sicily be moved to the Aegean to assist the Greek and Balkans campaign. Malta remained open to the British for the supply convoys of the Royal Navy and the RAF. The British not only had the use of Malta for supplies but also the supply route through the Suez Canal.

Rommel had little support. Italy seemed to have lost interest in the desert war and Hitler seemingly had no immediate ambition to capture either Egypt or Malta. Lt.-Col. Prendergast had been given charge of LRDG activities and his patrols were constantly sniping at the supply lines of the Afrika Korps, and the Tobruk garrison was still sending out sorties to harrass Rommel's troops. The German advance had been halted and the Allies were securely back at Baggush so the Germans were no better off in the spring of 1941 than the Italians had been in the spring of 1940. All in all, Rommel's rapid advance had been something of a hollow victory, despite German newspaper reports to the contrary.

It is probable that during the summer lull between seasons 1940/41 and 1941/42 Auchinleck had greater peace of mind than Rommel. Hitler had invaded Russia in June 1941. Germany was becoming hard pressed in Europe. Britain had not been invaded and in reality only half of France had been occupied. Rommel in the desert was something of a sideshow in Hitler's mind, a gimmick to show Mussolini that German troops could succeed where Italian forces had failed. The truth was: Rommel in the desert was simply a German-inflicted smack in the eye for cocky Mussolini. That, in 1941, was the extent of Hitler's interest in the desert.

Churchill, on the other hand, regarded the desert as a decisive battleground and this explains his impatience with first Wavell and then Auchinleck and their 'slow 'n' easy' approach.

Operation BATTLEAXE had been a failure so Auchinleck was not going to be pushed into further action until he had a reasonable chance of success.

Auchinleck had a new commander, General Sir Alan Cunningham, a man who had achieved astonishing success in Kenya and Somalia. (He thus was able to fight alongside his brother, the Royal Navy's Admiral Sir Andrew Cunningham, in the Middle East campaign). Alan Cunningham's Number Two was Lt.-General Ritchie. Together they commanded the 8th Army. Lt.-General Godwin-Austen commanded XIII Corps and, to complete the usual three-pronged attack, Lt.-General Norrie commanded XXX Corps.

Auchinleck's operation was going to be named **CRUSADER** and its objective would be to destroy Rommel's armour, relieve Tobruk, and regain Cyrenaica.

Whenever Auchinleck visited his front-line troops at Battle HQ he, like Wavell, was properly dressed in full uniform but his relaxed attitude and pleasant manner endeared him to his men and the visits were very much 'at ease'.

November 1st came and went and it was not until November 16th that Auchinleck decided to move. Churchill had kept his promise and supplied his Desert Commander with troops, supplies, tanks, and arms, so on the morning of November 17th there were over 100,000 men at the front, 600 tanks, and 5,000 assorted vehicles.

There was an element of shambles about the opening thrust of Operation CRUSADER, and the weather could not have been worse. There were thunderstorms and heavy rain on the night of November 17th which bogged down vehicles. Units lost contact, there were cases of men being run over by tanks or trucks, springs and axles broke far too easily, and the amount of petrol required to get the 8th Army moving was colossal. What made fuel a major worry was the fact that at least three petrol carriers overturned and almost 2,000 gallons of fuel seeped into the sand.

Churchill sent a message to his desert troops: *"For the first time British and Empire troops will meet the Germans with ample equipment and modern weapons. The battle will affect the whole course of the war . . ."* Morale in the desert was high.

It needed to be in the face of the worst weather recorded there for many years.

The foul weather did give Auchinleck's men one advantage: Rommel never imagined anyone would start a war in such awful weather conditions. No German aircraft observed any British movement so on November 18th the 7th Armoured Brigade reached its objective (Gabr Saleh) without opposition. The 4th Armoured Brigade was more than 10 miles east of Gabr Saleh, and the 4th Indian Division had reached 'the Wire', and the New Zealand Division was a few miles inside this border between Cyrenaica and Egypt.

When Rommel did receive reports of an Allied 'push' he, understandably, assumed it was one more of the many reconnaissance or LRDG patrol 'pushes'.

General Strafer Gott led the 22nd Armoured Brigade towards Tobruk hoping that he would have enough success for General Cunningham to order the Tobruk garrison to attempt a breakout and join forces with their comrades. This order had to be carefully timed to ensure success and there was so much chaos in and around Tobruk that it was difficult to form an accurate picture so it was decided that the time had not yet arrived for the relief of Tobruk.

On November 20th Rommel finally realised that he was up against a major attack, and the fighting which followed was the fiercest yet seen in the desert.

The situation remained very confused for several days. In the melee the 7th Armoured Brigade was almost wiped out and this was a terrible loss, but the New Zealand Brigade captured the HQ of the Afrika Korps. Unfortunately the C-in-C, Generalleutnant Ludwig Cruewell, was not among the captured staff. When he heard of this Allied success he sent an army to fight the 5th South African Brigade and inflicted very heavy casualties on them. The whole of Rommel's forces were now fighting like devil-possessed furies.

By November 22nd it was still impossible to say who was gaining the upper hand. Cunningham became indecisive and sent a message to Auchinleck asking him to come to the front line and make a decision about advancing in the face of Rommel's terrific onslaught. Cunningham felt that the Allied operation might have to be abandoned to save unbearable losses of men and equipment. He was wilting under pressure.

Auchinleck surveyed the position. He reasoned that Rommel too would have problems, so he asked Cunningham to carry on as planned. Rommel was indeed also suffering heavy losses, and Hitler was not giving him the support Churchill had supplied to Auchinleck. The Allies felt confident enough to press forward.

Rommel, like a boxer losing on points and knowing that only a desperate knock-out blow will defeat his opponent, gathered his exhausted troops and decided to attack Auchinleck's forces head on, a direct face-to-face confrontation with the object of pushing the Allies back over 'the Wire' and into Egypt. Then he would pound the troublesome port of Tobruk and capture the garrison. Rommel's personal pride was at stake over Tobruk.

Auchinleck was unmoved by Rommel's desperation. Like the aforementioned boxing match Auchinleck knew he only had to remain standing to win on points. But, he and his Desert Rats had to withstand the attempted German knock-out blow.

On November 26th Auchinleck, feeling that Cunningham was not quite the right man to tackle Rommel, put Major-General Ritchie in charge.

The fighting increased in intensity, Tobruk remained in siege, losses were high, but Ritchie knew that he had more in reserve than Rommel.

The tide turned Ritchie's way when Tobruk was relieved on November 27th and the 2nd New Zealand Division joined hands with the holders of the Tobruk garrison.

Soon it was December and the Germans could expect no reinforcements from Europe. Auchinleck and Ritchie patiently gathered their battered forces, reorganised them and prepared them for victorious action. The Tobruk success restored the morale of the Desert Rats and they flexed their muscles for the final push towards Benghazi.

By December 7th Rommel realised that his brave and bold frontal attack had failed and he made plans to withdraw. He had lost over 800 tanks and armoured cars, 127 aircraft had been shot down, and among the 10,000 prisoners were three German Generals.

Rommel was disappointed too by the lack of solid support from the Italians. General Gambara, for example, was supposed to use two divisions to assist Rommel but the Italians took no part in the battle. Rommel complained to Mussolini who immediately put all Italian forces in the desert under Rommel's control. However, when Rommel asked for a steady stream of supplies Mussolini said that this could not be guaranteed because the Mediterranean was so dangerous. It was a fact that 14 of 22 Italian ships destined for Rommel had been sunk by either the RAF or the Royal Navy.

One bloody month (the night of December 16/17th) after Auchinleck had begun his attack Rommel accepted that absolute withdrawal was necessary if he wanted to avoid annihilation. Ritchie was the one who was slowly and painfully advancing, and Strafer Gott with the 7th Armoured Division was also showing great skill as an Allied Commander in desert warfare. Then there was Major-General Bernard Freyberg (three DSOs and a VC in World War One) with his New Zealand Division, and also the charismatic and fast-becoming-legendary Jock Campbell with the 7th Support Group and the famous 'Jock columns'.

Even though Rommel was retreating the fighting remained bitter and the two sides shared the abomination of desert thirst, itching neck sores, sweat-stained collars as rough as sandpaper, cuts which would not heal, the most primitive sanitation, fear, cold nights, rain and sleet, and the inevitable build-up of dead bodies, stench, aching bellies, unexpected minefields and unexpected air raids. Only comradeship held the respective armies together as 1941 ebbed to a close; Rommel's men retreating, Auchinleck's men advancing towards Benghazi.

A report by Cyril Joly spoke of *carnage as far as the eye could see, dead and dying strewn over the battlefield, frightening to see, awesome to behold.*

Rommel and Ritchie, attempting the classic desert manouvre of 'encircle and capture', found that with the terrible weather and the many individual advances and retreats taking place that this technique was impossible and only pandemonium reigned. Sheer exhaustion was slowing down both sides.

During December Ritchie could not press too hard on the retreating Germans because of petrol shortages, the exhaustion of the troops, and inadequate equipment. (In particular, the tanks needed thicker armour plating).

On December 15th Rommel reported to Berlin that his men were showing signs of weariness, equipment and munitions had broken down, and withdrawal was necessary. In the battle of wills between the Germans and the Allies the deciding factor had probably been the relief of Tobruk. Rommel had placed so much on its capture that his failure to achieve this almost certainly boosted the morale of the Allies and deflated that of the Afrika Korps.

The Kings Dragoon Guards, some of Strafer Gott's men, Derek Rawnsley's desert patrol, and a few others, enjoyed Christmas dinner in Benghazi. When Wavell, a year earlier, had arrived in Benghazi the inhabitants had welcomed the Allies because their arrival freed the Libyans from the occupation of their homeland by the Italians. When Auchinleck's men arrived the reception by the locals was muted because the war had done so much damage to their beautiful city.

Operation CRUSADER fizzled out because munitions, fuel, tanks, and stores, had become completely disorganised and inadequate, plus the fact that each side had fought the other to a stalemate, a stand still.

Rommel was bitter because he felt that he had been defeated by his own government and that of Italy. Some supplies and men from Germany and Italy were now reaching North Africa, but it was too late.

It was estimated that at the start of Operation CRUSADER the Allied forces were 118,000 and the Axis forces 119,000.

The Allied losses were 17,700 (killed, wounded or missing) against the Axis 38,300 (k.w.or m.) and these look advantageous to the Allies until further examination reveals that the Allies lost 2,900 killed against 2,300 by the Axis, and that of the 38,300 Axis (k.w.or m.) 30,000 or more were safe as prisoners of war. All in all it had been a costly operation for

MASSACRE AT ALAMEIN?

Auchinleck, albeit one which supplied headlines of desert victory which Churchill found encouraging.

There had been many heroes, Allied and German. One man who represented the tough dedicated fighters on both sides was *Jock Campbell and he was awarded the Victoria Cross.

It was now 1942.

Rommel and Auchinleck needed to plan for the next encounter. Each sensed that it would be decisive. Operation CRUSADER had shown them what was needed for complete victory.

Auchinleck needed a planned withdrawal. He was stranded too far from his base in Alexandria. It would be unwise to attempt (January 1942) to reach Tripoli. That was Rommel's base, and Auchinleck needed to draw the German 'Desert Fox' as far from Tripoli as possible thus making the German/Italian supply lines almost a thousand miles long, open and vulnerable to the destructive sniping of the LRDG patrols, the RAF bombing, and the Royal Navy bombardment of enemy ports plus the sinking of Axis shipping in the Mediterranean Sea.

AUCHINLECK

*On February 23rd 1942 Jock Campbell, VC, was killed in a desert car accident.

CHAPTER FIVE

The Secret of Alamein.

(This report on Egyptian local history is to show why Auchinleck had to bear in mind the political situation and also that he began, unknown to the outside world, preparing the 'Alamein Ambush' as far back as January 1942).

The year 1942 was the turning point during World War Two. The three years, 1939–41, had belonged to Hitler but the next three, 1942–45, from the Allies point of view, saw the end of his megalomaniac dream of world domination; his Third Reich which was 'to last for a thousand years'.

In reviewing the war in the desert during 1942 it must be remembered that no military operation anywhere in the world that year can truthfully be judged in isolation. The war really was world-wide; extending from the Pacific to the Atlantic, from the Far East to the Middle East and Europe and to America. War in one theatre invariably affected decisions in other war zones.

The finale of the 1941/42 desert war under Auchinleck and the beginning of the 1942/43 operation at Alamein under Montgomery have to be seen in worldwide context to understand the significance of the decisions made by Churchill affecting the desert war.

The British Prime Minister, for instance, knew that if he could form an alliance with Stalin and Roosevelt it would be a triumvirate which Hitler could not possibly defeat, so, many of the 1942 decisions which Churchill made had the wishes and needs of Stalin and Roosevelt in mind.

The big name now (1942) to emerge from the desert battles was, of course, Alamein.

Not many people outside Egypt had heard of Alamein and newspaper reports and books which in 1941/42 described Alamein as merely *a stopping point where the desert train halted to take on water, where there was nothing but a shed and a few empty oil drums, a dot not even named on maps of the Western Desert,* was accepted blindly by readers the world over. Alamein was a 'nothing' place, one of no significance, until October 23rd 1942, of course.

In Egypt, however, there had been much talk of Alamein, especially among LRDG and other desert surveyors, the Egyptian Army, King Farouk, the major land owners, and Government officials. The talk was about a canal at Alamein.

There had been canals in Egypt ever since ancient times, even a Suez Canal had been considered several times over the centuries. The Pharoahs had rejected it once, and on another occasion the Venetian Republic and the Sultan of Egypt planned a Suez Canal but the Turkish invasion of 1517 put a stop to the project, not to be taken up again because it was realised that a Suez Canal would destroy Alexandria as the most important port for overland trade between the Far East and Europe. A Suez Canal would only be of advantage to Britain and European countries. The Suez Canal which opened in 1869 had been forced on the Egyptians by the British and French. The Egyptians viewed a canal at Alamein with much more favour.

Contemporary (1940s) plans for a canal at Alamein had to be kept as secret as possible because there was no telling what effect it would have on the level of the Mediterranean Sea and this would alarm Italy, Greece, Turkey, and even as far west as France and Spain. The Suez Canal (115 miles) joined one sea to another so there was less fear of a drop in sea level but a canal at Alamein would take water from the Mediterranean Sea into a sub-sea-level area covering at least 7,000 square miles with a circumference of 600 miles, and ranging from 435 feet below sea level to 1,000 feet thus creating an inland sea of gigantic size. The area to be thus flooded, or partially flooded, was known as the Qattara Depression.

Irrigation canals could make fertile the vast area of Egypt's Western

MASSACRE AT ALAMEIN?

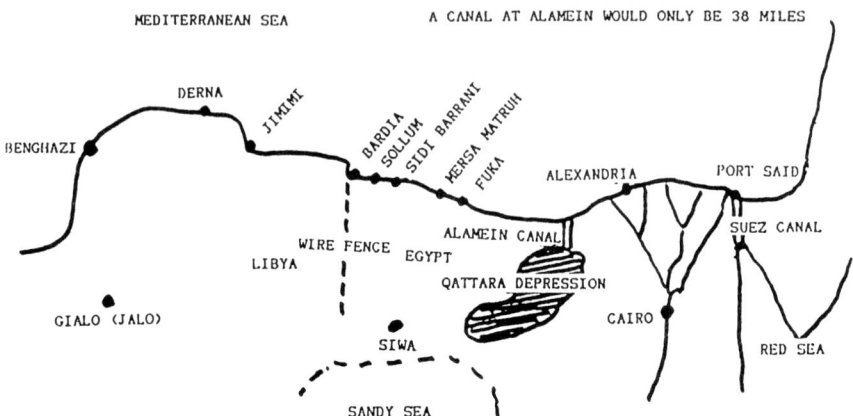

ANCIENT EGYPT WAS KEEN ON BUILDING CANALS

AN OLD CANAL FROM ALEXANDRIA JOINED THE NILE AT RAHMENIYEH.. JOURNEY BY WATER TO CAIRO 180 MILES. (1855 CAIRO-ALEXANDRIA RAILWAY CONSTRUCTED, 128 MILES). THE CANAL WAS BUILT IN 1819 BY MUHAMMED ALI. OPENED IN 1820, WORKFORCE 250,000 OF WHOM 20,000 DIED. THE CANAL WAS KNOWN AS THE MAHMUDIYEH CANAL.

IN HIS BOOK, 'LIBYAN SANDS', RALPH BAGNOLD WRITES OF A DR. BALL WHO SUGGESTED 'A TUNNEL' TO FLOOD THE QATTARA DEPRESSION. THIS WOULD BE IDEAL FOR THE CREATION OF HYDRO-ELECTRICITY AS WELL AS THE MORE OBVIOUS USE FOR IRRIGATION. DAVID STIRLING WROTE OF ANOTHER SCHEME TO FLOOD THE QATTARA DEPRESSION USING WATER DIRECT FROM THE RIVER NILE. MANDELL'S SCHEME TO USE WATER DIRECT FROM THE MEDITERRANEAN SEA WAS THE MOST EXCITING AND WAS MUCH TALKED ABOUT DURING WW2. WHEN ROMMEL WAS DRIVEN OUT OF NORTH AFRICA MANDELL'S GERMAN PARTNER (OTTO) IS BELIEVED TO HAVE BEEN RESPONSIBLE FOR SENDING IN AN HUNGARIAN TEAM TO SURVEY THE POSSIBILITY OF A CANAL. WHEN DAVID STIRLING WAS A PRISONER IN COLDITZ (1944) HE WAS ASTONISHED TO LEARN THAT THE GERMANS THERE HAD A COPY OF A PLAN TO FLOOD QATTARA. WAS THIS THE MANDELL/OTTO AMERICAN/GERMAN PLAN RUMOURED IN CAIRO CIRCA 1942?
IT TOOK DE LESSOPS 15 YEARS TO OBTAIN THE FINAL PERMISSION TO GO AHEAD WITH THE 108 MILE SUEZ CANAL.
IS IT NOT TIME THAT EGYPT (WITH AMERICA, GERMANY, BRITAIN, OR ANYBODY!) DID SOMETHING ABOUT AN ALAMEIN CANAL, ESPECIALLY AS EGYPT'S POPULATION IS GROWING BY 1.2 MILLION A YEAR! B.L.

The Alamein Canal Project

Desert and make this historic area once more a 'land flowing with milk and honey'.

David Stirling was one of many who knew of the Alamein Canal scheme. It was not a new idea. His friend and LRDG colleague Ralph Bagnold wrote about it in his book *Libyan Sands*. In this book Bagnold writes of a Doctor Ball who had suggested 'a tunnel' to flood the Qattara Depression and, so as not to frighten the Mediterranean countries who would not want their ports left high and dry, Doctor Ball planned to use water from the Nile. Stirling and others could see hydroelectric possibilities from water falls, in some cases 600 feet, in the rocky salt-infested uneven area.

The lure of the canal never left David Stirling and even in the 1960s his South African company Gemsbok was still dreaming of fertilising the Western Desert with a network of irrigation canals.

Stirling was captured by the Germans in 1943 and was moved from place to place until he ended up in Colditz in August 1944. In between planning escape schemes he was astonished to come across 'a paper' in the prison written by 'a German' describing how the Qattara Depression could be flooded!

This 'German' might have been the companion of Jack Mandell, an American representative for an oil company. Mandell found no oil under the sands of the desert (unlike in Saudi Arabia and other Middle East deserts) but the idea of irrigating Egypt's desert by constructing a canal caught his imagination and with typical American enthusiasm he and a German friend (living in Cairo as a Swiss national and known as Otto) obtained an audience with King Farouk and were granted Royal support to pursue the matter. Mandell is supposed to have obtained a promise of American financial support and Otto a promise of German know-how in dam and canal construction. Rumours also had it that several members of Egypt's group of 'Free Officers' (founded 1939, and from where Nasser and Sadat later emerged) were also interested.

There was to be a dam built on the coast at Alamein to control the flow of water to the Depression 35 miles inland.

The Egyptians in the know were pleased with the idea of American finance and German construction. With the patronising British and the arrogant French removed from Egyptian land the Americans and Germans would make a welcome change.

Despite Egypt's fanatical desire for recognition of its full independence the country knew that its economy needed foreign support of one kind or another. American aid would do very nicely, thank you. And German too. Had not Hitler already promised King Farouk that he and Egypt would be the Islamic leaders of the Arab nations? Furthermore, the Arabs in Palestine were rather pro-Hitler. The German Fuhrer had granted asylum in Berlin to the Grand Mufti of Jerusalem. When the British marched into Iraq in 1941 to prevent a pro-Nazi coup the Prime Minister, Rashid Ali, also found sanctuary in Berlin.

Initial secret work at Alamein could begin under cover of the 1942 desert battles. Surely, it was excitedly argued, 'we Egyptians are within our rights in building an *Alamein Line* to defend Alexandria, the Suez Canal, and Cairo? What about *The Siegfried Line, The Maginot Line, The Mareth Line?* Were not these concrete barriers built to defend national territory'. Alamein would be even better because whereas armies could go round the three defence 'Lines' mentioned, Alamein would be an ambush because the sea and Qattara would make it impossible 'to go round'. And this, the argument went on, could be given as explanation if a foreign country enquired about suspicious activities at Alamein. Working on the coast with large quantities of concrete for a dam could be passed off as building concrete bunkers for the military.

Cairo, city of rumours, thus had one more subject to ruminate on while taking coffee in Groppi's or puffing contentedly on a hookah in some street cafe.

The German Afrika Korps believed, like most people, that the Qattara Depression was impassable but the LRDG knew that this was not so, as did the Arabs. For centuries the desert Arabs had used the Kaneitra Crossing, and the LRDG had successfully explored and crossed this great inland dead sea.

One patrol commander, Captain C. Mather, published an article in the *Royal Geographic Journal* in April 1944 and from this it is obvious that much research and survey had gone into the study of Qattara by mining consultants, surveyors and geologists.

MASSACRE AT ALAMEIN?

Early in 1943, with the Allies now well away from the Western Desert, a Hungarian-led expedition was reported scavenging about in the Qattara Depression.

Although the interest was wide-spread in Egypt there was opposition to the canal, mainly by groups who favoured something being done about controlling the flooding and drought caused by the Nile. These people wanted any money that was on offer to be spent on a new Aswan Dam. In 1954 Anthony Eden was so obsessed with a desire to get rid of Nasser that he would not support the Aswan Dam project, preferring to wage war and in doing so let in the Russians who offered help to Egypt. Work on the canal never began.

There is still hope for the Alamein Canal because things move slowly in Egypt. The Aswan Dam was not completed until 1970, and it is called the Nasser Dam. The man-made sea there is the second largest in the world. The Qattara Sea would be the biggest ever, an Eighth Wonder of the World.

In 1954 Nasser survived an assassination attempt and soon after that he nationalised the Suez Canal, costing the British and French millions of pounds in lost revenue. Eden led a disastrous war against Egypt in 1956. (Eden should have spent some years in the desert before he meddled in Middle East affairs!). This brief essay into Egyptian history is given because it had a material effect on the course of action made by Auchinleck. So, to return to the Desert War of 1942.

Desert Commanders and Cairo-based officials, bearing these rumours in mind, realised that Alamein was the perfect place for Battle HQ. Baggush had served well when the war had been between Wavell and the Italians either side of 'the Wire', but Alamein would be perfect in the 1942/43 season, the one the Allies in the desert knew they would win if the promised new tanks and guns arrived.

It was only 65 miles from the lights of Alexandria. City leave for desert soldiers! What Paradise! The Alexandria 'Fleet Club' open to all forces, theatres, cinemas, nightclubs, girls, and the red light exhibitions of Sister Street! It almost transformed desert life into something approaching military civilisation!

And, the shorter the supply lines the stronger the army. Auchinleck would be a mere 65 miles from base. Rommel would be 1,000 miles; Tripoli to Alamein. His Bouerat and Benghazi ports could be bombed by the Royal Navy and the RAF, and the LRDG and SAS patrols could destroy his supply dumps and air and transport depots wherever they were deposited.

Best of all, from Auchinleck's point of view, was the fact that Alamein was more than a defence line, it was an ambush in which Rommel would be trapped. His Panzers could not move in the Qattara Depression and this factor was worth twenty divisions to Auchinleck. Rommel's troops could not sail round the northern end of the line. Auchinleck would have enough troops and minefields to create a solid line across which Rommel would be unable to cross. If he advanced to Alamein he would be trapped. But would he advance so far? The 'Desert Fox' had a reputation for being very desert-wise.

Supplies, aircraft and men had been promised to Auchinleck by Churchill despite the fact that the British Prime Minister was also doing his best to satisfy Bomber Harris and, in addition, to remember the needs of India and the Far East. Churchill did not let the Desert Rats down, and the promised equipment began to arrive in Egypt during 1942.

Even so, Churchill was not impressed with Auchinleck when newspaper headlines spelt out British retreat and German advance in the desert. Auchinleck remained cool, believing firmly that the headlines later in the year would be of the kind Churchill looked for.

Auckinleck knew that it was going to take a 'third season', 1942/43, to successfully clear North Africa of German and Italian forces and, as the Cairo rumours insisted and the desert surveyors knew, Alamein was to be the flash point of the next great battle.

But so far the outside world had not heard of Alamein, and the War Cabinet in London failed to understand the significance of Auchinleck's choice of Battle HQ and his gradual withdrawal during the first half of 1942. ('twas ever thus; in 1922 Lord Milner had warned that it was a mistake to judge Egypt from London.)

Back home there were other operations which were of more obvious benefit for the Allied cause and which caught the public's eye.

For example, the January 1942 arrival of American troops in Northern

Ireland who were welcomed by the Secretary for Air, Sir Archibald Sinclair, greeting them with, *"your safe arrival is a gloomy portent for Mister Hitler!"*

When the news broke it raised the hearts and hopes of the British who were gasping not only at the desert reverses but also at the advancing Japanese in the Far East and the advancing Germans in Russia. In February 1942 Singapore fell. Also in that month Sir Arthur Harris became Head of Bomber Command. This was better news.

Arthur (Bert) Harris, who soon became known as Bomber Harris, (Churchill's sobriquet) put an interesting theory to Churchill. The Germans had started 'terror bombing' cities. Now that the American Air Force was available to join the RAF bombing raids (USA by day, RAF by night) why not terror bomb Germany in return? Thousand Bomber raids could so terrify the Germans that surrender might be achieved without the need to open a Second Front in Europe with its possible loss of a million lives.

Bomber Harris, being in England, was in constant touch with Churchill. Auchinleck was out of sight and almost out of (Churchill's) mind. England had become a different place since 1939. The British worked together as never before, or since. Churchill and the Royal Family were adored icons. There was a wartime cameraderie, but it was of necessity more frenetic than the laid-back cameraderie in the desert.

So it was Harris who had Churchill's ear, not Auchinleck.

In February 1942 Harris was talking to Churchill about bombing Germany into submission: "We will systematically take apart the Third Reich, city by city, street by street, until the Boche surrenders. Attack the morale of the German people!"

This was the kind of fighting talk Churchill admired. But he wanted facts.

"Can you win the war?" he asked.

"Give me four thousand Lancasters and accurate navigational equipment and you will not need the Russians or a Second Front. No more trench warfare. Devastate their industrial cities. Terrorise them from the air. Thousand bomber raids! Bomb round the clock!"

"But can you win the war?" Churchill repeated.

"Yes, by July 1943."

MASSACRE AT ALAMEIN?

This was a definite promise and Churchill was intrigued. England did not want a return to the World War One mentality where large numbers of men died simply to gain a few hundred yards of Flander's field. 'Up, over the top, and at 'em!' This Battle of the Somme mentality was too much within living memory for the British to relish a futile 'Charge of the Light Brigade, the gallant six hundred, guns to the right of them, guns to the left of them, onward rode . . .'. A Second Front *would* be as lethal as the Charge of the Light Brigade. If thousands of men were to die in Europe better those of the enemy than our own men. We had been fortunate to save so many at Dunkirk, there was no desire to throw their lives away needlessly if a Second Front could be avoided.

Churchill gave his consent to Harris's 'terror bombing' and by the end of May Harris was ready.

He had raged at Lord Beaverbrook, Minister for Production, that he wanted aircraft *here* where the real war was taking place, so, stop sending aircraft to the Middle East. Bomber Harris succeeded in geeing-up aircraft production and the design of better navigational instruments. Events in the desert must have seemed as small fry to Churchill and his War Cabinet in bomb-conscious London.

Now for the order Harris's pilots had been waiting for.

"Cologne. Tonight! Let's wipe it out!" Harris said.

There were 1,455 tons of bombs dropped with 40 planes lost, (3.8%, and Harris had predicted a 4% loss)

The raid caused much damage to built-up areas and this bombing of innocent civilians in Cologne and in other cities also bombed by Harris, such as Hamburg, Dusseldorf, Chemnitz, Dresden, the Ruhr, and most important of all to Harris, Berlin itself (Hermann Goering had promised the Berliners that no RAF bomb would ever fall on their city) became a moral issue.

Churchill, nevertheless, revelled in American-style headlines such as BERLIN HIT BY 350 COOKIES, and as huge fires burned in Berlin a popular song hit the air waves, 'Berlin or Bust'.

The resultant toll of civilian deaths hit the conscience of churchmen and created arguments about ethics. In defence Harris angrily replied that war was a complete breakdown in civilisation and did not need 'ethics', and his RAF chaplain responded with equal anger that it was not the ethics of bombing so much as the bombing of ethics.

In World War One the philosopher Bertrand Russell had preached that if the Germans invaded Britain they should be treated amiably, (a philosophy upheld by others such as Gandhi, and the tennis player Bunny Austin). However, Bertrand Russell in 1942 gave his support to Bomber Harris's tactics. The bombing of British cities during 1940/41 had brought home a few truths about war.

In June Eisenhower was chosen to be in charge of forces in Europe and the Americans soon showed that they preferred to bomb military installations such as factories, oil depots, railways, and this put a curb on Bomber Harris's exploits. Maybe because the Americans had not had their cities bombed they took Bertrand Russell's World War One view rather than his more realistic World War Two opinion *apres la bombardement.*

As 1942 progressed and Churchill read of Auchinleck retreating nearer and nearer to Alexandria one can imagine what the Prime Minister's thoughts were.

The psychological division between those in the desert and those at home was growing ever larger.

The Desert Rats had no worries about the ethics of bombing civilians and built-up areas; there were no civilians or built-up areas. Desert battles *could* be fought under what Bomber Harris referred to as 'Haigh rules of Combat'.

Neither Rommel nor Auchinleck saw the desert war in 1942 as the rest of the world did. Let the headlines scream out news of Rommel's 'victories' and Auchinleck's 'defeat'. Rommel and Auchinleck viewed the situation far differently. However, having described in this chapter the war as seen from London in 1942 one cannot blame the world for believing that Auchinleck was being defeated.

Rommel, even as he advanced, knew that this was not so.

CHAPTER SIX

The Censored *Asthenia of Rommel.

German military Historian Werner Haupt records in *North African Campaign* that in January 1942 Rommel and his staff officers planned in secret to attack Auchinleck and *as a result neither Hitler and the German Supreme Command, nor Mussolini and his Commando Supremo, knew anything about it.*

For Rommel to keep his plans secret from the British is understandable but to deliberately keep them secret from his own higher command suggests that the Desert Fox knew that Hitler and Mussolini would not approve.

So why did Rommel take a chance and attack? The answer is simple. Five supply ships carrying German tanks had got through to Tripoli. These tanks had advanced eastwards towards the battle area as Rommel had retreated. When the two forces met it presented a miraculous opportunity for Rommel. The weather was settled, too. One did not need to be the Brains of World War Two to decide to use this unexpected gift of reinforcements and snatch victory from defeat.

The Afrika Korps struck on January 21st and advanced towards Auchinleck's front line. A few days later, as Rommel's plans became evident, Marshal Cavallero (Italy) and Field Marshal Kesselring (Germany) arrived at Rommel's HQ in the desert to see what was going on.

*Asthenia: loss of strength.

MASSACRE AT ALAMEIN?

Italy's written response was handed to Rommel, *At all costs drop this offensive and withdraw*. Germany's instructions to their wayward desert commander would have been similar had not Rommel vehemently argued with Kesselring that the world headlines proclaiming Auchinleck's desert victories had been bad for German morale and if the Afrika Korps recaptured Benghazi then the headlines of that coup would offset those which had favoured Auchinleck in December 1941. This new influx of tanks should be used, surely.

Seeing Kesselring hesitate Rommel offered another plum.

"And Tobruk, would that not be another great feather in Germany's cap?"

Kesselring, Rommel's senior officer, finally agreed because these two places were in Libya and not Egypt, and it would be a triumph if Rommel regained them. Hitler would love to condescendingly hand Cyrenaica back to the beleaguered Mussolini with the patronising injunction, "Here's part of your Empire back, now look after it!" It had been on the premise of helping Mussolini out of trouble that Germany had gone into North Africa in the first place.

Auchinleck during the early months of 1942, withdrawing to the east, was not too worried. Rommel's influx of tanks spread over the thousand miles from Tripoli to Alamein made far less of a fearsome spectacle than if kept in tight formation. The LRDG patrols could pick them off from time to time.

Neither Italy nor Germany had any plans now to invade Egypt because relations with King Farouk, the Egyptian Government, and the Egyptian people were quite cordial. Egypt was as pro-Italy and pro-Germany as it was anti-Britain.

Italy had not only lost Cyrenaica but also its East African Empire of Somaliland, Eritrea and Ethiopia. The unorthodox British officer Lt.-Col. Orde Wingate had successfully engaged the Italians and on May 5th 1941 the noble-looking Emperor of Ethiopia, Haile Selassie, had returned to Addis Ababa in triumph, five years after the Italians marched in and The League of Nations had failed to see justice done to the dethroned Emperor.

Wavell had master-minded the downfall of the whole Italian Empire.

41

MASSACRE AT ALAMEIN?

By 1942 Mussolini's popularity in Italy was at an all-time low and Il Duce, as he called himself, had no ambitions for further military defeats. The Italian people wanted peace. They looked on the Nazis as gangsters and had no desire for the 'new order' promised by Hitler.

Italy certainly had no desire now to wage war with Egypt. King Farouk's four palaces were full of Italian servants, so much so that the British Ambassador believing them (correctly) to be Italian spies ordered Farouk to get rid of them.

It so happened that Sir Miles Lampson's first wife had died and he had recently married Jacqueline, a beautiful young Italian girl (not much older than his own daughters) from a well-known Anglo-Italian family, the Castellanis. The new *Lady Lampson lived at the British Embassy in Cairo. King Farouk (amusingly, to most people) met one piece of affrontery with another by telling the Ambassador's messenger, "Tell Lampson to get rid of his Italian and I'll get rid of mine!"

The Italian people loved the Egyptians, and vice versa. (From the time of his exile in 1952 to his death in 1965 Farouk lived in Italy). In short, in 1942 Italy had no heart to support any invasion of Egypt by the lone-wolf, Erwin Rommel.

Germany, too, was on friendly relations with Egypt and would gain nothing by military occupation. Hitler, knowing of Farouk's love of fast cars, had sent as a wedding present in 1938 a super-charged Mercedes Super-SSK convertible, the sort of car most young men could only dream of possessing. (The British sent a couple of Purdey shot guns, a dull gift compared with Hitler's glamorous offering).

One incident above all others stood out in the Lampson/Farouk enmity.

Early in 1942 the King, very popular with many senior British officers, was enjoying a holiday in the desert. In the King's absence the Egyptian Cabinet, under severe pressure from Lampson, withdrew diplomatic recognition of the Vichy government. The King, on his return, was outraged and the Prime Minister, Sirry Pasha, resigned in face of the King's fury.

* *My 1943 diary: Fri. May 7th. British Embassy, danced with Lady Lampson. (It must have been in a 'Paul Jones' or a 'Gentleman's Excuse-Me' dance.) B.L.*

MASSACRE AT ALAMEIN?

Lampson too was furious. How dare the Boy King go against the British Ambassador's wishes!

Then followed one of the most bizarre incidents even by Cairo's colourful standards.

Lampson, on February 4th, (a week before the King's birthday, incidentally) filled the courtyard of Abdin Palace with tanks and troops, and with Victorian gun-boat diplomacy he entered the palace and ordered the King to appoint a Prime Minister of Lampson's choosing, in the event, Nahas Pasha who had been dismissed as Prime Minister by Farouk in 1938. Sirry Pasha was Farouk's uncle by marriage.

Knowing Lampson was on his way Farouk ordered his staff to behave politely, correctly, and with regal dignity. Farouk, not risking giving Lampson a reason to depose him, said, "I am appointing Nahas Pasha as my Prime Minister. This interview is now ended!", and with a dismissive wave of his arm Farouk left the room.

King Farouk had saved face before his own staff, but Lampson had won the day. At one stroke the bullying British Ambassador had produced a lame duck King and an impotent Prime Minister. One could *feel* the hatred in Cairo for the British Ambassador and his boss, Churchill.

The Egyptians would at that time have welcomed Hitler with open arms. Their neighbours, the Palestinian Arabs, would also have welcomed the Germans. Who better to curb the Zionist ambitions in Palestine? Hitler might have enjoyed a Palestinian holocaust. There might never have been an Arab-Israeli war.

Of such stuff are political dreams made.

Dreams or not, Hitler could have got all the Middle East co-operation he wanted without firing a single bullet.

In 1942 Rommel was on his own. The Fuhrer only wanted a few good headlines, and that is the reason he left Rommel out in 'the blue'.

It should not be thought that British and Egyptian troops did not get on quite well. It was pointless for an Egyptian soldier to tell a British soldier to get out of Egypt because the British soldier would immediately reply, "Look, mate, give me a ticket to Blighty and I'll go now!" The attitude of almost all Egyptians was that they did not want British people in Egypt as members of an occupying force or of a 'Protectorate', but if they came back as visitors they would be very welcome.

In his book, *In Search of Identity,* Anwar el Sadat writes of the excellent behaviour of the troops. "The British kept to their Clubs and the Egyptian soldiers to theirs."

If King Farouk happened to be in a nightclub and some British entered (other than Lampson, of course) he never minded their company. Indeed, his student years in England in the 1930s had taught him to enjoy British humour. Such apocryphal stories as the British soldier briefed to give evidence in a car accident he had witnessed said, "There was a car with three wogs in it . . ." The officer stopped the soldier and explained that this was very disrespectful, especially as one of the gentlemen in the car was King Farouk himself. In court the soldier gave his amended evidence, "There was a car with King Farouk and two wogs in it!"

It was always good humoured in Cairo.

Unlike in the terrible time Europe was having, and especially in Russia and the Far East where horror stifled humour.

Hitler did not have the man power, or the planes, to support a major desert war. He was in the same trouble as Napoleon had been 130 years earlier, namely, discovering that a long-term invasion of Russia brings the invader up against two enemies; the Russian people, and the Russian winter. That is why Rommel could not be given adequate air cover. Hitler had no spare aircraft or aircrews to send to the desert. He needed every plane available for Russia, Europe and Great Britain, especially with Britain's rapidly increasing air power. There was also the arrival of the Americans on the European scene, and French resistance was rising in strength. Hitler had made Laval a virtual dictator in France, but how loyal could Laval be called when on the one hand he thanked Hitler for clearing France of British soldiers and on the other hand he told the British that he would adopt a 'hands off' attitude if the Allies landed in France.

Goebbels, in charge of Nazi propaganda, was desperate for material in 1942 and like a drowning man he clutched desperately at Rommel's 'victories', blew them up out of all proportion to their real military value, so much so that Hitler was delighted to have some good news and to celebrate the re-capture of Benghazi he made Rommel a Colonel-General, and Goebbels succeeded in making Rommel a number one National

Military Hero, an icon to admire and follow. Kesselring had been wise to allow Rommel to attack.

Not a great deal of significance happened in the desert during February and March, and Rommel guessed correctly that Auchinleck was not so much retreating as re-grouping before starting a major push later in the year. Rommel sent a message to Berlin that a summer or autumn offensive by the British was inevitable (the 1942/43 season!), Rommel thereby admitting that the German advance did not spell 'victory'. He pleaded for arms and other necessary supplies so that he could at least take Tobruk and have something to show for his efforts. He further impressed on Berlin the need for Germany to capture or subdue Malta.

The combination of German air strikes and Italian Naval bombardment was a joint effort by the Axis to neutralise Malta. If this could be achieved then there was some hope of getting supplies to Rommel. During April 1942 some 6,700 tons of bombs were dropped on Malta, and the island was awarded the George Cross by King George. Gradually the RAF gained supremacy and Malta held firm. This boded ill for the supplies hoped for by Rommel. (After over one thousand air raids on Malta Hitler gave up and decided to use the aircraft in some other theatre of war.)

Neither Rommel nor Auchinleck wanted a stultifying 'All Quiet On The Western (Desert) Front' so skirmishes continued, with Rommel advancing and thus lengthening his supply line, and Auchinleck withdrawing and shortening his.

Rommel took Tobruk on 21st June 1942 and Goebbels made such a thing of this that Hitler promoted his Desert Fox to the rank of Field Marshall.

In truth, however, the Afrika Korps was in a very difficult position because it was short of supplies and had very little in the rear. Behind Auchinleck there were in Egypt over a million men and new arms and better equipment arriving all the time. Furthermore, the Free French under General Leclerc offered their full support to Auchinleck.

German historian Werner Haupt stated that during the summer of 1942 Rommel lost faith in Hitler's leadership. Haupt further stated that by now Rommel began to suffer from the mental inertia which affects all but the genuine desert nomad when left in the desert too long without a break. The

MASSACRE AT ALAMEIN?

British referred to this as being 'Sand Happy'.

The translation of a captured letter written by a German soldier not only shows the German disillusionment in the desert campaign but also the German awareness that the British were coping very well 'in the blue'.

" . . . *bitter thought that I should be stuck out here, perspiring like a pig, eating food I would not give to my dog, and constantly covered by flies. I had hoped to be in England. That is what we were promised. Why can't we beat the English in England instead of this terrible desert? The Tommies seem to understand the desert and wander about like damned gypsies, not bothering about the heat, dust, sand and flies.*

Their Allies: Australia, New Zealand, and South Africa, are tremendous fighters. Our Allies, the Italians, are lazy incompetent fools. They even shoot at us, by mistake, but I suspect they don't care who they shoot at.

The Tommy patrols are impossible. When they are short of food they raid our camp and steal ours. Rommel tells us things will get better when we have air control. But where is the Luftwaffe? Yesterday Tommy planes bombed our supply dump . . . all our coffee, and 40,000 litres of wine, beer and spirits."

Rommel knew that his desert campaign had no future in it, no purpose other than his personal pride and Hitler's need for good headlines. Shortly after his promotion Rommel wrote in a letter to his wife, "*There are no more medals to be won in the desert*".

In July 1942 Haupt wrote of Auchinleck's ascendancy, "Auchinleck had clearly gained the initiative on the battlefield", and this is confirmed by Rommel himself who recorded, "Our forces are now so weak in comparison with the steadily growing strength of the British that we are to count ourselves lucky if we can go on holding our line." (Reported in *North African Campaign* by Haupt and Bingham.)

In the middle of September Rommel went on sick leave to Germany and was not surprised to find that other senior officers were losing faith in Hitler. In strict secrecy he joined their ranks. General Stumme was left in charge of the Afrika Korps,

In August Churchill met Stalin in Moscow. That made a headline Goebbels did not want. There was now Churchill, Stalin and Roosevelt on the same side. That trio caused alarm in the upper echelons of the German

MASSACRE AT ALAMEIN?

officers. Plots against Hitler were planned.

Many plots failed and there was a wave of arrests by the Gestapo. In 1943 the full extent of the 1942 revolt became clear. The young officer Fabian von Schlabrendorff had smuggled a bomb on to Hitler's aircraft but the bomb failed to go off. The famous July 20th 1944 bomb which almost killed Hitler exposed the strength of the German Resistance. Rommel was part of that Resistance.

Who would have imagined that less than two years after the Battle of Alamein, Field Marshall Erwin Rommel, Germany's National Hero, would be given by Hitler the choice of committing suicide or facing a trial for treason!

Hitler made an offer; if Rommel committed suicide he would be given a state funeral, cause of death suitably hushed up, and his fame as a National Hero still intact for Germans to keep as an example. His widow would be given a state pension and keep her home.

If Rommel refused, and so exposed his lack of faith in Hitler, he would be tried and killed.

When we remember how the German Secret Service tortured victims, and how Admiral Canaris, for example, was hanged until unconscious, cut down, asked how he liked his foretaste of death, and then hanged again, we can appreciate Rommel's decision to shoot himself on October 14th 1944. The state funeral which followed was a complete phony, put on to impress the flagging morale of the German people.

Rommel's press conference in Berlin on October 3rd 1942 (the Battle of Alamein had still not taken place because of a remarkable change of plan by Churchill) was also a sham because Rommel knew his one thousand mile long supply route was a sitting duck for the marauding LRDG and other patrols. His allies, the Italians, would far rather be British POWs than fight under Nazi NCOs, and he realised that he was ambushed with little likelihood of crashing through the Alamein Line. He said all the right things, of course, to satisfy Goebbels and Hitler, but Rommel was in no hurry to get back to the desert. Auchinleck's Alamein Line had meant a fullstop for Rommel.

Egyptian opinion on the reliability of the Alamein Line was divided. There were those who knew that Auchinleck was in such a strong position that Rommel could not possibly win. But there were others who were under the spell of the Desert Fox and had doubts and were therefore frightened of Cairo being invaded; Mussolini riding in on a white horse, and all that that meant! The Italians knew Rommel could not now win and they cancelled their secret order for North Africa Campaign medals with Mussolini and the pyramids on one side and winged victory on the other. The British it was who struck the Victory Medal, the Africa Star for their Desert Rats!

Invasion was something Cairo had never felt necessary to contemplate. (It is ironical that Cairo did not need a blackout until *after* the war, in 1946)

The invaders in 1942 were not 'Italians' or 'Germans' but thugs known as 'Fascists' or 'Nazis'. For the first time there was an element of fear.

When the Afrika Korps was driven back on October 23rd many in Cairo felt a sense of jubilation that 'Britain had saved Egypt from invasion!' The euphoria did not last long and very soon Lampson and Farouk were back at their bickering and the Free Officers at their planning and plotting.

Churchill, visiting Cairo at the beginning of August, could surely see for himself that Auchinleck was on to a winner. One estimate (Haupt & Bingham) of front-line totals was given as: Auchinleck *500,000-plus men and 1,800 tanks (mostly new), Rommel 120,000 men (including disinterested Italians) and less than 200 tanks (entirely old). Why then wait until September 9th? The British Prime Minister wanted action. Strike while the iron is hot. Victory was there for the taking. Why wait?

Unfortunately for Churchill his commander, Auchinleck, considered it too hot in August. Did the Prime Minister not realise how unbearable was the heat inside a tank in August? Did he not realise that the Alamein caravan had to travel one thousand miles to Tripoli and the 1941/42 season had shown how carefully such an excursion had to be planned: oil, petrol, water, food, spares, et al. Had not Churchill understood the painful lessons of the previous advance?

Auchinleck insisted that September 9th was the earliest date to start the big push. Everything was in place. His valuable 'Second Front', the private

---

*Tom Pocock's book on ALAN MOOREHEAD also confirmed these figures. pp 146/147.

MASSACRE AT ALAMEIN?

armies plus LRDG and SAS, were under the unified control of a staff cell called 'G Raiding Forces'. The backup forces were ready. Morale was high, despite reports to the opposite. It was certain that the weather in September would be cooler than in July or August and less treacherous than in November. September seemed to be a perfectly rational choice.

But it meant too long a delay for the impatient Prime Minister.

On August 8th 1942 Auchinleck was relieved of his post.

It was the end of Auchinleck in the Western Desert but, although the world did not yet realise it, it was also the end of Rommel.

ERWIN ROMMEL

CHAPTER SEVEN

How 'Private Armies' Were Formed

In order to understand the importance of the Back-up force the Private Armies provided the following chapter is written in the First Person. It shows how a natural leader (in this case F/O Derek Rawnsley, RAF), obtained permission and then handpicked his men. Later all the LRDG and SAS Patrols were organised from GHQ, and these patrols controlled the whole of the desert inland from the coastal road from which the Axis troops never wandered. B.L.

The desert railway clanked its way to a halt at Baggush (Battle HQ, Western Desert) one torridly hot Friday evening during the summer of 1941.

I alighted and with several other Forces' personnel I reported to the sentry at the barbed-wire entrance to compound. The area seemed strangely quiet after my twenty months in the frenetic bustle of swinging Cairo. My luggage was of the briefest: toothbrush, razor, and a few 'akkers' (Piastres; Egyptian money) to spend in case there was a desert 'Naafi'. I could not see any canteen, but it did not matter because I was only there for the weekend.

I explained this to the sentry, "I'm from RAF Intelligence, GHQ Cairo, and I am here to relieve the Camp Surveyor who has been given weekend leave."

"Take that tent over there," said the NCO.

MASSACRE AT ALAMEIN?

I was shown to a tent in the RAF section (I was really 'Army', Royal Engineer, Survey, on loan to the RAF) and presently an Army NCO brought me bedding, eating irons, plate and mug, and wished me an enjoyable weekend's swimming. The golden powdery sand, sprouting small clumps of desert shrub, fell gently down to the Mediterranean coral-edged coastline. The British Royal Family, and the privileged rich of Europe, had enjoyed pre-war holidays at nearby Mersa Matruh. Indeed, Cleopatra herself had bathed in these sublime waters. Within the hour I was diving off a smooth stone pedestal into about eight or ten feet of water. A huge shoal of fish, each pure white creature being about nine inches long, scattered as my splashing dive disturbed their evening nesting.

The two tents closest to mine were respectively occupied by Flying Officer Derek Rawnsley and Flying Officer Patrick (Lord) Kinross, RAFVR. Patrick was an author and journalist, and had succeeded to the family title in 1939.

By the following Friday I had come to two conclusions: one, I was in for a long weekend because my absent colleague Lacey had not returned and two, Derek and Patrick were very friendly companions to have 'in the blue'.

They were amused at my predicament and wanted to hear how it had come to be. The simplest explanation was to briefly relate the chronological steps which had led me to Maaten Baggush.

"1937 Ordnance Survey, 1939 Royal Engineers Survey, January 1940 Abbassia Barracks, Cairo, and then sent as surveyor and draughtman to RAF Intelligence GHQ (Grey Pillars) Cairo. Summer 1941 sent to relieve fellow-RE Lacey at Baggush who, I was told by 'Busty', the civilian Head of our section at 'RAF Intelligence, Maps, GHQ', had been given weekend leave."

"This Busty fellow didn't say Lacey was returning to the desert after his 48-hours pass, did he?" Derek laughed. "Perhaps Lacey is on his way home."

"I don't know where he is," I replied. "We call him Red Lacey because he reads books about Communism."

"That's it," said Derek, "he's on his way to Russia."

I think Derek and Patrick were also amused when I told them that I believed the only people working on the Survey were those whose names began with L. I shared a GHQ drawing office with Lambert, my piano-duet partner on Radio Cairo was Loewenthal, my fellow athlete in the British Empire International Athletics Team was Littler, my dining companion in Cairo was Latham, and later, when I was sent to help the South African Survey at Maadi in 1942 my close friend was Lavarack. A Survey friend of mine, Dai Morgan, being one step further in the alphabet, had just missed the cushy billet at GHQ and was sent to Greece where he was captured and died in an accident in a German POW camp. How fortunate that my name was Leach and not McLeach!

The drawing office at GHQ was manned by civilians, officers and other ranks, each doing similar professional work, but, the officers and civilians had the use of certain hotels and clubs 'out of bounds' to other ranks. It seemed palpably unfair that because I had volunteered to serve my country I should be barred from, to mention just one famous watering hole, Shepheards Hotel. Through friends I 'had the use of a flat' in Sharia Antikhana, a minutes walk from Groppi's coffee house, and by changing into civilian clothes I was thus able to accompany my fellow civilian surveyors and several new-found Egyptian and English civilian friends into the full range of swinging Cairo. I thus gained a wonderful understanding of this fascinating city. Mind you, I had to be careful because the Forces magazine PARADE had twice published my photograph, once as a pianist and once as an athlete, and the Military Police (Redcaps) were keen to see that all troops were 'properly dressed'.

Patrick was interested in the flat because he rented one in the Kasbah area of Cairo. He had it well furnished and he told me that he often enjoyed wandering in the narrow streets as he wore full Arab dress. The Daily Express journalist Alan Moorehead also lived nearby. David Stirling, hero of the LRDG, loved Cairo. His brother Peter had a flat in the Garden City area and David was frequently in that neighbourhood. It seems that David had an English nurse as a friend and if he had been up too late and had drunk too much he rushed to her hospital in the morning and she gave him a few whiffs of oxygen which not only sobered him up but also filled him with energy for the rest of the day, so the story goes. Now we know where he got the energy to organise the LRDG (Long Range Desert Group) whose romantic exploits were beginning to rival in public popularity those of the RAF fighter-pilots, the romantic 'Brylcream Boys' of Battle of Britain fame.

It was a strange experience, my first few weeks in the desert. I felt quite at home. Not everybody did. Derek and Patrick seemed comfortable enough in their surroundings. Patrick, by some magic, had the ability to turn up unexpectedly from some of his many trips to Alexandria with a few bottles of really cool Stella beer.

"Like a beer, dear boy?", and Derek would reply in their RAF jargon, "That would be wizard!" If I happened to be around (i.e., not swimming or sleeping) Patrick would hand one to me. Incidentally, there *was* a canteen at Baggush.

Weeks passed delightfully by and confirmation of my confinement to Battle HQ was settled when my mail began to arrive from Cairo. So, I was not expected back. Oddly enough, I was very happy. Of course, so far I had not been asked to do anything. The swimming at Baggush was absolutely wonderful, or should I say, 'Wizard!'

Patrick Kinross flew regularly to Alexandria and started a newspaper and books service for the front line troops. Derek became thoughtful, as if he was planning something. He disappeared for days at a time. Patrick and Derek were not men to be idle for long. Derek's wife, Brenda, was in the WAAF and he managed to get her posted to Cairo.

One day an NCO arrived at my tent and handed me a large scale map of Cyrenaica and one of the Egyptian Desert.

"Your mate left these behind. Camp Commandant says to give them to you," and I was also handed a couple of pencils and a rubber and a few sheets of blank cartridge paper. At least I was now 'open for business'.

Derek and I spent many hours talking about poetry and literature, art and music, and thanks to Patrick's regular supplies we had plenty of books and magazines. I read the complete works of Shelley, followed by Keats, with much more enthusiasm than I had at school.

Derek Rawnsley was a big man in many ways. He had a touch of the Lawrence of Arabia about him, he loved fine things, he was a natural leader and he showed an interest in people. He would rather, for instance, ask me about my life than tell me about his. I had to tell him about

MASSACRE AT ALAMEIN?

international sport in Cairo. Until Mussolini declared war in June 1940 the Mediterranean countries such as Italy, Turkey, Greece, Syria, Spain, Egypt. Morocco and Palestine, were free to continue with normal sporting fixtures, especially football and athletics. The British Empire entered into the spirit of these fixtures and I ran in most of the international meetings which took place in Cairo during the first half of 1940. Derek had censored my letters home (to save time and possible loss en route) and thus knew a lot about my private life.

When we had exhausted the arts and sport he began to ask me about the survey work I did, or could do if anybody asked!

"Bob, if in a moment of madness they did give you some work to do here, what sort of stuff would it be?"

I had come to Baggush without any instructions but I presumed the following to be the most likely of my duties and I explained them to Derek.

"Well, if your RAF pilots sent in an overlapping strip of air photos I could view them stereoscopically with my bare eyes and that would indicate any camouflage. Third dimension. Stereoscopic. Anything of height would stand up but anything merely painted to look like emplacements or dumps would remain flat. I could draw a target map. There is also tachiometry. That is used in an emergency, where the surveyor goes out armed with nothing more than a pencil and a piece of paper and returns in half an hour with a recognisable map of the area. From this a route could be planned. For more exact work minefield positions have to be accurately plotted, showing safe lanes through the minefields which the RE Sappers have checked. While we surveyors are in the desert we have been asked to place the sand surface into one of three groups: hard sand which could take tanks and on which planes can land, medium sand on which troops can walk, and soft sand in which a walker would sink to the ankles or even deeper, in other words, the dangerous 'Sandy Sea' in which men and camels and vehicles could disappear. From these reports a comprehensive map is constantly being revised in Cairo."

"What if you got lost in the desert?"

"If daytime, stay put. I guess. Get your bearings when the sun sets in the west. Then walk northwards. At night. Lie low during the day. Look for the North Star. Boy Scout training, eh? Follow the star. Bound to hit the Med. sooner or later. Nothing else you could do, is there? Depends how much food and water you have."

"Or someone finds you."

"Yes. There's always that hope."

I was soon to discover why he was quizzing me so thoroughly.

Although I remember Derek Rawnsley well I find it difficult after all these years to describe him. He was a big man, fair hair, casually dressed, well spoken, very good-looking, tall, but above all I remember his kindness and his interest in people. He was the kind of man you could accept as leader no matter how independent and self-confident you yourself might feel. There was no reason at the time why I should memorise details of the man; colour of eyes, height, weight, and so on. What I clearly remember is 'his presence'. He was a man who had 'presence'. He did not dominate or bully or 'pull rank' (he was an officer, I was not, but never once did he make use of this seniority).

Derek did one more of his disappearing acts, and I swam and read (I was 'into' Lawrence of Arabia now) and rested until he returned. This time he brought back a real surprise: three armoured 15 cwt. trucks, each with an Australian driver, and also an Army officer who was an expert in bombs and guns. A naval Lieutenant Commander Wilmott joined us. Derek introduced me to his motley crew and then explained, "I had a Hell of a job persuading GHQ to let me raise this Private Army. We need a navigator. How about it?"

"Me?"

And that is how Derek raised his Desert Patrol, by constantly nagging at the Big Wigs in Cairo. He called us the LRI PATROL, LRI standing for 'Long Range Intelligence'. I never bothered to ask Derek if he had got permission for me to join. It wouldn't do to ask too many questions. After all, how could Baggush survive without its busy camp surveyor!

I shared a truck with Australian driver Mick. He was a customs officer in Melbourne and when I mention that in England custom officers and ordnance surveyors needed to pass the same Civil Service exam, it indicates that Mick and I came from the same work background. We were both in our twenties and we became very good friends. He said I was his 'sidekick', a word which entered our desert vocabulary. Mick had a tiny camera and I still have lots of photos he took. (Many of the photos I took were stolen after the war when I was burgled.)

Derek's sidekick was Jacko, an Australian corporal, very craggy and tough. He looked as though he was in his thirties. His experience included sheep farming and gold mining in Queensland. He was used to living in the open, and he became the patrol's cook. Derek and Jacko rode in the 'wireless truck'. Jacko said of Derek, "I'd follow that man through Hell with a candle!"

The third Australian was Arthur Rowe, a very quiet man, broad shouldered and stocky, mid twenties. He shared a truck with the Army lieutenant (I forget his name) who was to show us how to shoot, throw grenades and fix bombs. This officer was tall, willowy and like Arthur, a very silent man. These two kept very much to themselves. Arthur was a garage mechanic and had the same ability as the lieutenant in taking things to pieces and putting them back together again. They made perfect partners.

Derek handed each of us a sandy-coloured duffle coat (which after the war I gave to my father, a merchant seaman), a revolver (which I had stolen from me in 1943) and ammo, a pair of goggles, and a pocketful of hand grenades. Because I was the navigator I was also given a compass. It was a beauty.

"Sorry about the binoculars. Very poor. They keep the best at Gezira to follow the horse racing!" Derek quipped.

"Don't need 'em," growled Jacko of the Plainsman's long-distance eyes, "you can see for twenty miles in the desert!"

I still had the large scale maps Lacey had left behind, and the pencils and rubber, but Derek gave me some spare maps on which to mark our desert forays as we went. Rations, water, petrol, spares . . . we were ready for a dummy run!

We moved to another part of the Battle HQ site, placed the trucks in shape of three sides of a rectangle, spread a large dark tarpaulin over the trucks and thus built what we hoped marauding enemy aircraft would take for an Arab tent. We now had communal sleeping quarters. Goodbye private tent! It was now groundsheet and blanket roll, and six men under one roof.

Derek needed to fly back to Alexandria. He had made a shopping list of extra requirements. He called to me to jump into a truck (Mick's) and Derek drove to where an aircraft was standing. He alighted and got into the cockpit, calling to me to take the truck back.

"I can't drive. What'll I do?"

'Oh, just drive the bloody thing!" and the aeroplane taxied off.

Using basic knowledge I put the car in first gear and drove back without daring to change gear. Mick had been watching from our tent and laughed as I pulled up, still in first gear.

That, I supposed to myself, was one of Derek's initiative tests.

"You'll have to show me how to change gear," I said to Mick.

"OK." he said, and that is how I passed my desert driving test. In Civvy Street I needed two attempts before I was allowed out on my own! However, this was the desert and when we eventually went behind enemy lines the drill was that in a scramble the first one back to the truck did the driving.

We gave ourselves a 48-hour pass and drove to Cairo where Derek introduced us to his WAAF wife, Brenda. Then, back into the blue.

Next we had to devise our own training on a dummy run. We drove off into the blue singing, 'We're OFF to see the Wizard, the wonderful Wizard of Oz!'

We worked out that our best plan, if attacked by air, would be to stop, jump out of the truck, and disperse left, right and centre, so that the enemy air-gunner couldn't shoot us all at the same time. We practised this a couple of times.

Each time we stopped I plotted on my map the distance and the compass bearing we had travelled, thus navigating with elementary dead-reckoning. We were driving in straight lines except when a wadi or dune made alteration of course necessary and this I charted on my map.

"Get it right or we'll never find our way back to Baggush," Derek said.

There were plenty of empty four gallon petrol cans (oblong; about 20" × 12" × 12") lying around in the desert. Stanley Humphrey, RAF, in his book, *Press On, Regardless*, describes how these cans were used in pairs to reclaim water, filtering every drop of dirty water. The lower tin had its top cut off and the upper tin had its base pierced with small holes. The top tin was filled with large stones, smaller stones, straw and sand. When filtered the water was clean enough to use for washing or shaving.

We in the patrol decided that once we went 'on ops' we would grow beards (mine made me look like the Laughing Cavalier).

While still on our self-imposed training run Jacko made one of the four gallon cans into a stove. At one end he cut a 10" square and at the other a 5" square hole. He placed the 10" hole into the wind which, having only a 5" exit, built up pressure. The top of the stove was cut away about 12" × 8". There was plenty of scrub in the desert and this was packed into the tin, lit, and placed windwards. It worked perfectly and Jacko could make a fry-up on his stove while the primus stove was used to boil water for tea or coffee.

Rations were plentiful even if it did look as though they might be monotonous: baked beans, bully beef, flour, Machonachie's tinned stew, and things which the Army referred to as 'biscuits' ('biscuits' was also the name given to the three square mattresses given to troops to sleep on and sceptics said the only difference between the two types of 'biscuit' was the size). We also had marmalade (South African), chocolate, tinned fruit, cigarettes, beer and whisky, tea, sugar and coffee, the latter three being excellent bargaining ingredients to exchange for chicken, eggs, fresh fruit and veg from the desert Arabs. We swotted up our Arabic for this important desert activity, bartering.

The Italians had changed the word 'petrol' into desert language 'benzine' (this happened because some Italian pilots would walk into a British camp and give themselves up. "Mafeesh benzine!" they would say with a fatalistic shrug but when the plane was examined the benzine was not 'mafeesh', the tank was still half full), and the Australians changed the word 'paraffin' into 'kerosene'. The three Aussies in the patrol called us 'Poms' and we called them 'Colonials' and asked them what it was like 'standing the right way up!' All very good natured.

We listened to the news at 6 p.m. As yet we had no trained wireless operator. LRDG patrols used the pips to set their watches for fixing their position on a map, using sextant and stars like sailors at sea. I could not do this, having no experience of using such navigational equipment, so Wilmott tried to give me a crash course in naval navigation. Derek said he would try and recruit a 'wireless op'.

MASSACRE AT ALAMEIN?

It was well into October 1941 when this dummy run took place. At night we discussed the purpose of our patrol and it seemed simple enough: to get behind enemy lines (the enemy remained almost entirely along the coastal strip) and attack dumps and depots, and then retreat. My job, apart from keeping track of our position, would be to up-date the desert map (akin to Ordnance Survey map revision, my peacetime profession); marking wadis, rock formation and, as I was to discover, forgotten and unplotted pyramids, forts, and long-dead terraced villages covered with drifting sand. Like the bed of the ocean, the expanse of the desert contained many fascinating relics of the past not recorded on any map or chart.

We also thought it might be a good idea that when we found an enemy arms or stores dump to attack it at dusk, one truck and one member would stay behind and the other two trucks would unload as much gear as possible into it so that a lightweight two-truck attack could travel all the quicker. For the person left behind, a duty taken in turn, it was an uncanny experience, to look around 360 degrees and see nothing but sand. (Later, this plan was abandoned because it limited our escape route. All three trucks would move in together)

Whenever we came across a group of Arabs they were invariably amiable and easy-going and on several occasions we bartered our goods for some of theirs.

We took our training dummy run seriously and felt that we belonged to a *corps d'elite* with our own David Stirling in Derek Rawnsley. When we got stuck in soft sand we cheerfully pulled the truck out, using shovels and one of the unstuck trucks doing the pulling. Derek had created a small band of dedicated men, each with a zest and an unconquerable self-confidence. Team spirit took the place of military discipline. We seemed to have no problems regarding food and water, and each of us seemed to be in perfect health.

A military survey had shown that Forces in the Western Desert were the fittest anywhere in the world, even back home in England. Ninety-five per cent were reported fit for duty at any time. No other theatre of war could claim such a high percentage, and nowhere else but in the desert could such freedom of action be allowed to individuals. We were in a wonderfully unique situation . . . free of all military 'bull'. Derek wanted each man to be an expert in his own field and this sense of equality, yet each depending on the other, was very strong.

One day we spotted a herd of about thirty graceful gazelle. Jacko shouted, "Shoot one and we'll have a roast dinner!" Our aim was anything but accurate but finally one of several hundred bullets shot an animal. The others then stood in a silently watching semi-circle as Jacko skinned the dead gazelle and hung it on the back of his truck to 'bleed'. As we drove off the semi-circle of animals watched, silent witnesses to the murder of one of their herd. When we looked back they were still standing in the distance, watching as we disappeared over a ridge of sand dunes. When we eventually stopped Jacko discovered warts on the flesh of the carcass so on his advice we did not risk eating it and the carcass was left for the kitehawks and jackalls.

We had been told that the probable date for Auchinleck's push would be some time in November 1941 (it turned out to be November 18th) so Derek wanted us back at Baggush by the first week in November. Much to my relief I directed them straight back to Battle HQ.

There was one problem, however. A 'wireless operator' was still needed to complete our team. Derek still needed a genuine 'wireless op.' and he enrolled teenager Bernie Stace, a genuine RAF-trained operator. He was by far the youngest man in the patrol.

There was one incident I still remember with personal satisfaction. My meeting with General Auchinleck.

It was early or mid November, 1941. Derek had disappeared (to collect as much of our shopping list as he could scrounge) and it was my turn to 'mind the shop'. Even though we were at Battle HQ we still guarded our precious stores and equipment by taking it in turns to stay on guard. I was having my last shave before growing my 'Desert Patrol beard' and had only a towel draped round my waist for modesty when some senior officers approached.

"Good day," said one.

Although I did not stop shaving and turn to face the speaker I was at least polite in tone when I casually returned the greeting, "Good day."

"Have you got everything you want?" the voice asked, still very gentle.

"Yes, I think so," and I turned my half-shaven face to look at the person so politely addressing me.

The controlled but frightened recognition in my eyes caused General Auchinleck to give the briefest of smiles. I could hardly stand to attention half shaven so I used the most polite voice I could muster and said, "the others are swimming, sir."

At that moment one of the two officers accompanying the General was holding a tiny desert animal and it disgraced itself by wee-weeing and this caused gentle laughter, and brought me a great sense of relief.

"Good luck with your patrol," General Auchinleck said and he and his aide-de-camp departed.

Derek returned and I related my frightening yet exciting meeting.

"Auchinleck's a good man. Wonderful understanding of the desert," Derek said. "His visit to Baggush probably means the push will not be long. We have work to do so we'll leave first thing in the morning."

By the time Operation CRUSADER started we were many miles south 'in the blue'.

As there were no politicians, police or ambassadors in the desert members of the LRDG patrols were called on to perform an amount of 'public relations' business with the desert Arabs, hence the brushing-up of our street Arabic.

For example, some Arabs believed a rumour that there was an ancient prophecy that whoever held Tobruk would hold Cyrenaica. This was alright in 1941 but later, in 1942, when Rommel was in Tobruk the LRDG went to great trouble to assure the Arabs that Tobruk was no great deal because Auchinleck knew what he was doing withdrawing to Alamein and 1942/43 would see the desert cleared of Germans and Italians.

Desert patrols also performed undercover work in releasing our own POWs before they could be shipped to Italy and then moved to Germany.

The Libyans, still smarting from Italy's occupation of their country, were encouraged to fight back and the Libyan Arab Force was founded and assisted by Captain John Haselden, of Anglo-Greek parentage and who had fluent Arabic. He was able to roam the desert as a Bedouin Arab, collecting important information. Valuable contact was made with the desert tribes and relations were kept on a friendly basis. This was important because we were fighting our way through their territory and we did not want them sniping at us while we fought the Germans and Italians. We were generous to desert Arabs whenever we could afford to be, and they gave us valuable information.

It was helpful to us to understand the nature and customs of the various tribes.

The proud Egyptian Arab (who liked to be called an Egyptian and not an Arab) was slow to indulge in laughter, and liked to completely subjugate his women. We saw for ourselves how the men and women occupied their own areas at the oasis of Siwa. King Farouk allowed the Siweans to follow their own version of Islamic belief. The Barasi Arabs allowed their women more freedom and were more prone to laughter. The Senussi Arabs hated the Italians who, even as late as 1942, were executing them under orders from Mussolini. Our desert patrols rescued many, especially in a purge between January and June 1942 when many Senussi Arabs were saved at the last minute from death at the hands of the Italians.

This goodwill meant that the LRDG could establish safe and well stocked bases at such locations as Siwa, Gialo (my personal spelling. I note others spell the name of the oasis as Jalo), and Landing Ground 125, from where the seriously injured could be flown to Alexandria or Cairo. The outside world knew little of this important desert activity. All that concerned the world press was the advancing and retreating along the coast, and on that was 'victory' or 'defeat' assessed.

Not all demolition raids were successful but even those that failed meant that the Germans could never relax, and we learnt lessons for future raids.

The Sudan Defence Force entered the desert to assist the LRDG.

Palestinian German-speaking Jews were keen to join up and to avoid going into the Pioneer Corps they volunteered for dangerous Desert Patrol work under Captain Herbert Buck. Their work was hazardous because on many occasions they wore Afrika Korps uniforms and were thus able to infiltrate deep into enemy lines. One such patrol was betrayed when a German spy infiltrated the infiltrators and they were wiped out when led into an ambush. Later on Derek's patrol were to operate in German uniforms and on one occasion were captured by the British. Their rude command of English soon convinced their captors that they were indeed a British LRDG patrol!

There were also French Commandos operating in the desert.

The numerous Patrols and Private Armies although working in haphazard fashion at first had by now become co-ordinated and well organised under such experienced leaders as Stirling, Bagnold, Laycock, Jock Campbell and Paddy Mayne. Desert Patrol action was planned to coincide with Auchinleck's CRUSADER operation starting on November 18th, 1941.

One brilliant idea (ruined by atrocious weather, and the fact that Rommel was somewhere else) was to capture Germany's national Hero, the Desert Fox, on the same day Auchinleck began his offensive, on November 18th.

The leader of this bold operation was twenty-four year old Lt.-Col. Geoffrey Keyes, holder of the Croix de Guerre and Military Cross, and son of Admiral Lord Keyes. Geoffrey Keyes trained his men on the beach near Alexandria. They planned to be taken by submarine to an area near to the coast at Beda Littoria, half way between Tobruk and Benghazi, and then to land by rubber dinghy. After the raid on the German HQ there, and the hoped for killing or capture of Rommel, a pick-up point had been arranged by the LRDG. There were six officers and fifty-three men involved in this daring and ambitious raid. The terrible weather and rough sea overturned several dinghies and it took the survivors six hours to reach the shore. The attack was spotted by the Germans and in the cross fire Keyes was killed. The chivalry which characterised the desert war was observed by the Germans who gave Keyes a burial with full military honours and taken by Rommel's own chaplain. The Germans appreciated the bold thinking behind the operation. To capture Rommel the very day Auchinleck attacked, what a triumph that would have been! Both Wavell and Auchinleck recognised that there were two fronts, the obvious coastal attack (or withdrawal) and the secret work of the Desert Patrols. Keyes was awarded a posthumous Victoria Cross.

No Allied desert commander in his right mind would go into battle against the Germans without the studied co-operation of the LRDG and the new SAS.

MASSACRE AT ALAMEIN?

In November 1942 Popski (Lt.-Col Vladimir Penjakoff, DSO, MC) who had seen long service with the LRDG patrols was invited to form a clean-up, or demolition, patrol. The patrol was ready by November 23rd 1942 and drove out of Cairo. Popski's navigator was an old friend of mine from the Ordnance Survey, Alex Petrie, serving as a Sapper, RE, Alec and I began our Ordnance Survey work on the same day, revising the maps of the environs around Lamberhurst, Kent, Christmas 1937.

Popski's adventures are recorded in his book *Popski's Private Army* published by Jonathan Cape in 1950. When the war in North Africa was over, 1943, Popski moved to Italy and wanted Alec to stay with him but the Director of Survey called Alec back to our Survey Base (Tura Caves, Massara, near Maadi, outside Cairo) and I am not sure where he went after that but I understand he was commissioned in 1943.

Those of us in Derek's patrol had Christmas dinner 1941 in Benghazi, arriving the same day as Auchinleck's advance forces, and then we spent New Year's Eve roistering in Gialo Oasis. Rommel was on the run, but Auchinleck had also run out of steam, as described in a previous chapter. The retreating Rommel was met by a column of German tanks which had landed in North Africa and with this gift from Valhalla, or wherever, he began his 1942 advance. At the same time the 'Alamein Ambush' was set up and this is where Rommel found himself trapped in the summer of 1942. A closer explanation of Auchinleck's Plan is explained in a later chapter.

At the beginning of 1942 our desert troops were re-grouped and Derek told me I had been called back to GHQ. Apart from the three Australians Derek's patrol was now exclusively made up of RAF personnel.

My weekend in the desert had spread into six memorable months. I was looking forward to returning to civilisation and had Busty said he regretted that my weekend had been so long I would have laughed the whole thing off, but, there was something in the way he said, "Ah, the warrior returns!", that offended me.

There are certain things we do instinctively, without thinking, like ducking to avoid being hit. With the same speed I replied, "I want to return to my unit!"

I did, my next assignment being with a South African Survey Unit in

MASSACRE AT ALAMEIN?

Maadi, and after first reporting to the 512 Survey Company at Massara, or 'the Tura Caves' as our mother HQ became known, I was sent with a Survey group to augment a South African Survey Unit based in the lovely village of nearby Maadi, a few miles south of Cairo on the Bab el Louk to Helwan railway.*

We were engaged in the making of target maps for the RAF Bombers and having strips of air photos regularly to hand I was thus able to closely follow the military action in the desert.

Rommel was now, spring 1942, advancing in the desert. Derek's patrol continued to operate behind enemy lines and did not disband until after victory at Alamein had been secured (November 1942). The three Australians were alright. Mick wrote to me and told me that he, Jacko and Arthur Rowe had returned to their unit which at that time was based in Palestine. He said the patrol had been shot up several times but no loss of life. Bernie Stace confirmed this many years later, in 1995. He died in September 1995, and I am still in touch with his wife, Dorothy.

Talk of military panic in Cairo in the summer of 1941 is nonsense. The world's newspapers suggested that Rommel was already as good as in Cairo. Such was not the case. I was in Cairo on my return from the desert and for those of us in the know there was quiet confidence that Alamein had become a battle we could not lose.

And someone else knew this to be so, Rommel himself, as the remaining chapters in this book will confirm.

My observations of the desert were two-fold: **one**, the surface of Cyrenaica was firm enough to carry a major assault force and this route could be used as a short cut from 'the Wire' to Benghazi if speed was essential. Rommel never left the coastal strip for more than a few miles. He did try to put a patrol into Gialo Oasis but the LRDG soon chased them out, and **two**, the weather inland was far more reliable than along the coastal strip. The Allies made use of the inland areas. Rommel never did.

While I was with Derek's patrol I did encounter one sand storm (Khamseen) which lasted for a couple of hours. We sat with our backs to the wind, heads covered, and as millions of grains of sand flew by at, say,

---

* *See picture, page 78.*

30 m.p.h., objects carried by the sand floated slowly past our noses at about 2 m.p.h. One such object was a 4-gallon petrol tin which sailed slowly past my face. (The British later copied the German 'gerrycans' for carrying fuel, much better than our 4-gallon tins, but they didn't make such good a-la-Jacko stoves, though!)

At no time did Rommel ever have control of the inner desert. That vast expanse of sand was under the control of the flotilla of Private Armies and Desert Patrols.

While the 8th Army was fighting along the coastal road in Auchinleck's CRUSADER push Derek's patrol was one of many making sure that Rommel did not use the firm ground of Cyrenaica to drive a flanking attack. (Such an attack would have been a much better bet for him than the failed full-frontal attack he did try in December 1941). Throughout the battle from November 18th to Christmas morning in Benghazi we did not see a single German soldier, German tank, or German plane. Nearer the coast we saw plenty of Axis wreckage; vehicles, planes, and small burnt-out tanks. No bodies. They had been decently buried. There was one giant Italian truck which the Australians boys tried to get started. The starting handle alone had three gears. However, it was 'kaput'. We helped ourselves to some tinned food, which proved to be delicious.

That Christmas 1941 we wondered if Rommel had opened a base at Gialo. It seemed the obvious thing for him to do. We went to investigate. There was not a sign of a German in or near that lovely oasis so on New Year's Eve we celebrated the arrival of 1942 in good Arab company, good spirits, and good heart. We slept well into the morning, and so did our convivial Arab friends.

Rommel could oscillate backwards and forwards along the coast road, Goebbels could scream that these were 'victories', Rommel could be made a field marshal and German National Hero Number One, but the secret truth was that we ruled the desert. Neither the Italians nor the Germans ever understood or occupied the desert as we did. When the LRI Patrol disbanded in November 1942 Derek Rawnsley returned to flying but I'm terribly upset to have to report that he was killed February 22nd 1943 on flying duties.

CRUSADER, beginning in November, had met cruel weather.

MASSACRE AT ALAMEIN?

September was a much better time to advance, hence Auchinleck's advice to Churchill to begin the push on September 9th, 1942. By then Auchinleck would have air superiority, new and better armoured tanks, superior numbers of men, arms and equipment. He would have the Mediterranean Sea and the Royal Navy to the north, his Alamein Line to Rommel's east, the impassable Qattara Depression to the south, and the LRDG, SAS, and others coming up behind Rommel.

Rommel's supply lines would be a thousand miles long, his stations would be as easy as sitting ducks for the marauding LRDG patrols. The Germans would not even have enough fuel to execute a full retreat or launch a major attack even if they wanted to. The Royal Navy and RAF were sinking the German supply ships in the Med. Their Italian allies were wondering how the Devil they could extricate themselves from the mess they found themselves in.

August would be too hot for Auchinleck's tanks. October and November would have unpredictable weather along the North African seaboard. September was the obvious and sensible choice to attack the exhausted and trapped Afrika Korps. Auchinleck had spent the whole of 1942 setting this up. September 9th (or thereabouts) was the ideal date to attack.

But, Churchill wanted an earlier date so Auchinleck was sacked.

Nevertheless, the truth remained that Rommel was trapped and his later actions in 1942 prove that he knew this. Rommel began thinking not of destroying Auchinleck but of destroying Hitler before the Fuhrer dragged Germany to complete destruction. Churchill plus Stalin plus Roosevelt? . . . too strong a trio for Hitler. Treasonable plots were afloat in Germany. We (certainly those with desert experience) in the Middle East firmly believed in 1942 that Alamein had become a battle the Allies could not lose, and 'we' included Rommel.

MASSACRE AT ALAMEIN?

Rear: 'Army Officer', Mick 'Jacko',
Foreground: Lt/Comm Wilmott RN, Derek Rawnsley RAF, Bob Leach RE.

The Wireless Truck.
The Wireless Operator.

Benghazi Cathedral,
Christmas Day 1941,
Arthur Rowe, Mick, Bob Leach.

Bernie Stace.

Derek's original seven included three Australians, one Naval Officer, one Army Officer, one RE Survey. In Nov. '41 Bernie Stace RAF joined as wireless 'op'. By March '42 the personnel of the LRI Patrol was exclusively RAF except for the three Austrailian drivers.

The Desert Patrol

CHAPTER EIGHT

GOTT STRAFE ROMMEL

When it was announced that General William 'Strafer' Gott was to take command in the desert following the dismissal of General Auchinleck, the journalists in Cairo began dreaming up sensational headlines;

MEIN GOTT! MEIN GOTT!
Rommel on the Run!

If it was a good headline Churchill wanted, well, he would have some eye-openers now!

The disappointment at Auchinleck's brutal sacking by Churchill was softened by the knowledge that the plum job was at least going to one of 'the desert veterans', in other words, someone who had played a leading role in setting up Alamein for the final victory in the desert.

The Allies now held practically all the aces. Perhaps the world's newspapers preached otherwise. That was because they had fallen for Goebbels' propaganda about the mystique of Rommel, plus the fact that neither Wavell nor Auchinleck were self-publicists. Thus, the situation at Alamein was not universally understood.

Not to worry! It would make the victory at Alamein seem all the greater and memorable when it happened on the carefully chosen date, September 9th 1942.

Churchill would then choose to forget that he had demanded a July offensive and had sacked Auchinleck for refusing to hurry. A headline such as

GOTT STRAFE ROMMEL!

would please Churchill when the Allied Advance pushed Rommel all the way back to Tripoli (1000 miles) and then across the sea to Italy. No one would care that the push had been 'delayed' until September. All those in the desert at the time, and those based in Cairo and in the Delta who had access to the true position, never doubted that this would be the outcome. Werner Haupt (p. 69 'North African Campaign') confirms that Rommel had no reserves to call on.

(Much of subsequent history wrongly clings to the view that Rommel was a force in the summer 1942 and that the Allied 8th Army was demoralised. For those who believe this, study the sheer weight of proven facts displayed in this book, written by someone 'who was there', either in the desert or in Cairo studying air-survey maps of the military situation on the ground.)

Strafer Gott played a prominent part in the desert war right from the first offensive by Wavell in December 1940. When the Desert Rats took Sidi Barrani from Graziani's forces and then advanced to Benghazi and completely annihilated the Italians in the desert Strafer Gott was then a brigadier.

Gott, therefore, knew how it all began, with Mussolini writing to Graziani on August 10th 1940 insisting that *'there are no territorial objectives. I am only asking you to attack the British forces facing you'* and Il Duce confirmed that he *'had no desire to capture Alexandria nor even Sollum.'*

Such was the lackadaisical Italian opening of their push into Egypt's desert.

It was not simply lackadaisical, it was chivalrous too.

On September 8th 1940 an Italian plane dropped a message-bag on the British Battle HQ giving the names of all British POWs and a report that a sergeant who had died had been buried with full military honours. Graziani wanted no hard feelings between the British and the Italians. The political leaders did not see eye-to-eye with the military leaders. It was a half-hearted Italian entry into Egyptian territory which occurred on September 18th 1940, completely devoid of set objectives, and it is possible that Mussolini was the only one wildly excited about the event.

Strafer Gott knew and understood the Italian hesitancy and was there when Wavell ordered his counter-attack and the Italians were driven clear of Cyrenaica and back towards Tripoli. In Operation COMPASS Gott's infantry was prominent (1st King's Royal Rifle Corps, 2nd Rifle Brigade, 1st and 4th Royal Horse Artillery).

Mussolini was embarrassed by this reverse, and was humiliated by Hitler's contemptuous offer in 1941 of *'Don't worry, we'll send a few Panzer Divisions and sort it out for you!'* Mussolini's attempted show of strength had rebounded in his face.

Having sent Rommel to North Africa Hitler then paid little attention to what the Desert Fox was up to. On June 22nd 1941 a German force of 3 million men invaded Russia along a 2000 mile front. That puts Rommel's role into true perspective. It meant Germany's desert war seemed like a minor border incident. Germany's desert war was fuelled by Rommel's personal ambition. He was a handsome dashing fellow who had swept into Paris and who had caught the eye of propaganda expert Goebbels. Rommel's personality suited the Western idea of 'desert romance' in the style of Lawrence of Arabia. If Hitler was unconcerned Goebbels watched events with interest. Losses in Russia could be offset by 'successes' in the desert.

In 1941, after the collapse of Mechili to Rommel, Wavell sent Gott (and his second in command Jock Campbell) to el Adem to form some sort of a screen to the south and east of Tobruk, a 50 mile semi-circle round Tobruk which needed to be held, mainly by the 11th Hussars. Gott and his men (main force 22nd Guards Brigade and four 'Jock columns') operated successfully, and to Rommel's acute discomfort, in the Halfaya Pass, Sofafi, Buq Buq and Sidi Barrani area.

In April 1941 Brigadier Gott used the typical 'Desert type attack', i.e., three-pronged, in the north the 2nd Rifle Brigade, in the centre 22nd Guards Brigade and 4th Royal Tank Regiment, and to the south his Armoured Brigade Group, Gott showing great skill as a Desert Commander. On May 16th he showed that he was brave enough to attack

71

superior forces but wise enough to withdraw when opposing such superior numbers made further attacks suicidal. He knew how to probe, investigate, weigh up the situation, and decide on balance whether to attack or withdraw. He would not have an unnecessary loss of life for a few hundred yards of sand.

In November 1941 when Operation CRUSADER began Strafer Gott (now Major-General) was in command of the famous 7th Armoured Division. Rommel was learning the facts of life regarding war in the desert during the summer months and in a letter to his wife Lucie he wrote, *'Dearest Lu, it was 107 degrees yesterday. Tanks standing in the sun go up to 160 degrees, too hot to touch.'* A pity he did not send a copy to Hitler and one to Churchill!

On November 16th and 17th when the 8th Army was on the move and became bogged down it was Gott who urged his Support Group forward (with the help of the 22nd Armoured Brigade) and on November 20th it was Gott who delivered plans for the Tobruk breakout. He also took charge when problems arose over waves of German Panzers which attacked on November 22nd during which there was heavy fighting and carnage before the British continued their advance on November 23rd.

No desert commander could claim superior experience 'in the blue' than W.H.E. 'Strafer' Gott. As far back as October 1938 Lt.-Col. Gott had commanded the 1st Battalion of the King's Royal Rifle Corps which had joined a multi-unit 'Mobile Force' based at Mersa Matruh, and which was to become the desert's elite force, The Desert Rats, the 7th Armoured Division, which gained fame and glory under Wavell and Auchinleck.

In December 1939 a Support Group, a development of the 1938 Mobile Force, came under the command of the then Brigadier Gott who had come to prominence the previous year when he was selected to train the 1st Battalion of King's Royal Rifles at the Citadel, Cairo, in the art of the desert warfare.

In 1941 William Gott took command of the 7th Armoured Division at Sollum near the border between Egypt and Cyrenaica. A member of the Royal Signals records that the new OC became known as 'Gentleman Gott' and that he was 'respected by all ranks'. Stories began to circulate about his generosity and charisma; how he would bring gifts from Cairo for the men in his HQ, and of an occasion when he stopped a rifleman digging a slit trench for a young officer and 'Gentleman Gott', educated at Harrow, made the officer dig his own slit trench.

In May 1941 Wavell's front line forces in the operation named BREVITY were under Brigadier Gott and included the Support Group of the 7th Armoured Brigade, 11th Hussars, 22nd Motorised Guard's Brigade, 2nd Royal Tanks, plus artillery and other units. BREVITY failed to relieve Tobruk but Gott's surprise tactics at Halfaya Pass allowed the troops to press forward until German reinforcements joined the Italian gunners and Gott retreated and re-formed to save suicidal losses.

Operation CRUSADER, November 1941, was Auchinleck's Big Push and the now-standard casual dress did not diminish the ferocity of attack and bravery under fire of the 8th Army. The dress of 'The Desert Rats' would have given any peace-time barrack square sergeant major a heart attack . . . 'You 'orrible little men might break your muvvers' 'earts but you'll not break mine!' But the 8th Army was a Desert Army. These were not 'Permission to speak, sir!' days. The men of the desert were allowed to think for themselves. They were free and easy, but no less dedicated. The conditions were unique in British military history. Wavell, Auchinleck, Gott . . . these men knew how to 'lead men' in the special environment of the desert. When it was all over, Churchill too understood: *It will be sufficient of any man to say, "I marched and fought with the Desert Army". February 1943.*

The Italians captured a certain Captain Clay of the 2nd Royal Gloucester Hussars in 1941 and were astonished to find him wearing . . . 'no badges of rank, a golf jacket, pink shirt, yellow silk scarf, green corduroy trousers, and suede shoes'. But this was exceptional, of course, even by Desert Rat standards.

Freedom of dress was sensible, really, because the standard battledress collar became like coarse sandpaper when sweat mixed with sand, the cuffs too, so difficult to heal desert sores formed and the pain was excruciating. Tropical uniform, too, was unsuitable because it was too cold at night. Remember that the 120 degrees at noon dropped to 80 degrees at midnight and with a fall in temperature like that anyone would feel cold. Suede shoes were marvellous for walking on sand . . . if you saved up enough

MASSACRE AT ALAMEIN?

money to buy a pair. There was no rationing in Cairo. New arrivals were quick to adopt casual attire (and to 'get their knees brown') and the dress was tacitly accepted by High Command in the Middle East.

The Desert Rats had enthusiastic support from GHQ, Cairo.

Rommel was not only denied enthusiastic support from Hitler but also from his own generals in the desert. The German Generals von Ravenstein and Cruewell in particular deeply resented Rommel's fanaticism, considering it to be selfish on the one hand and quite out of proportion to the whole German war effort on the other. The Germans were in the desert to patronisingly display Mussolini's incompetence and show off German military invincibility. Hitler never envisaged an invasion of the Middle East; and the Italians? . . . they had enjoyed a love affair with Egypt ever since the days of Cleopatra. This desert business was nothing more than a lovers' tiff, the soonest forgotten the better! I heard several Italians in Egypt express this view.

The attitude of the Italians gave Rommel a ready-made excuse for failure. As Ronald Lewin wrote in 'Afrika Korps' . . . *Rommel blamed the Italians all along the line.*

History shows that Rommel's command of the Afrika Korps suffered fits and starts.

In November 1941, when the Germans were near to Tobruk, the 7th Afrika Korps had been commanded since September by Lt.-General Cruewell who had shown rare skill as his men took on the British formations one by one and inflicted heavy losses.

It had been the 21st Panzer Division commanded by General von Ravenstein which had driven the 7th Armoured Division back, aided by Major-General Neumann-Silkou who commanded the 15th Panzer Division.

Rommel had led the 1941 attack on Tobruk with the 21st Panzer Division and despite having superior (in numbers) forces he had failed . . . *'leaving German occupants of Halfaya Pass under General Bach to their fate!'*, and that is written by a German historian! (Werner Haupt).

Haupt continued, *'The Desert Fox was beaten.'*

The point being made here is that the Africa Korps was not a one-man-band led by Rommel. He was, in reality, not the super German hero

Goebbels made him out to be. German 'victories' in the desert were not always of Rommel's making

During the 1942 German advance into Egypt Rommel was in ill-health both mentally and physically. It was kept secret at the time but post-war release of letters confirms that this was so. His men, too, were in desperate shape and Rommel wrote to Berlin on their behalf, *'the men are showing signs of weariness, especially as supplies have completely broken down.'*

Rommel was suffering from fainting fits and stomach disorder and his consultant in Germany, Professor Horster of Wurzberg University, stated that Rommel was not in a fit state to continue in command. But, Goebbels had made Rommel a hero, the Desert Fox, so he was ordered to remain in charge of the Afrika Korps.

He was a 'lucky' soldier, however. During Auchinleck's withdrawal to Alamein Tobruk was evacuated (it was now of no great value to the British. It would be risky for the Germans to use it as a port for receiving supplies because it was open to British naval and air attack and raids by LRDG and SAS patrols. The change of tenancy had been an excuse to promote the Desert Fox!). When the Germans entered Tobruk in June 1942 Goebbels hailed it as a tremendous victory and Rommel got the baton he wanted so badly, that of a field marshal.

While this pantomime was going on Auchinleck visited Ritchie at Baggush to discuss the Alamein Ambush. Ritchie's consequent withdrawal encouraged Rommel to advance deeper and deeper into Egypt, but the Desert Fox was far from pleased to be in this uncomfortable position. It was too much like being drawn into a dangerous No-Man's-Land. In July Rommel wrote to Berlin, ... *'our forces are now so small in comparison with the steady growing strength of the British ...'*

Maybe that was why Churchill wanted action in July 1942, but, with the metal bodywork of tanks rising to 160 degrees in the noonday sun! ... and a journey of 1000 miles to Tripoli the objective? ... surely Auchinleck was right to opt for September. Churchill was placing too much on the fact that Rommel was past his best. The Afrika Korps had other generals quite capable of being in charge: von Bismarck, Nehring, von Vaerst, Riller von Thoma, Stumme. (Kesselring, by the way, was busy in Russia, where Germany's real war was taking place.)

MASSACRE AT ALAMEIN?

Rommel might be at the peak of his fame but he was far from his peak as an active soldier. Ronald Lewin comments, *'Rommel was ill, weak in body and mentally distracted.'* and Rommel himself wrote to his wife complaining of a physical malaise.

He was always less fit and often more edgy and indecisive than his driving will allowed him to appear. Lewin continues, *'His will was losing control of his body.'*

And now, with the removal of Auchinleck, Rommel was faced with a new Leader of the Opposition, the renowned Strafer Gott. One wonders if Rommel remembered the World War One German slogan, 'Gott Strafe Engelland!' Rommel was at his lowest ebb, Gott would be at his peak of energy and enthusiasm for battle.

Then suddenly,

... the day after Gott's appointed to succeed Auchinleck, 7th August 1942, Gott's journalist friend Alan Moorehead had to report to the Daily Express the following terrible news that *'as Gott took off from a desert airstrip in a transport aircraft two German fighters returning from a sweep shot it down and Gott was killed.'* That, however, is not the full story. General Gott survived the actual crash and got out of the plane. It was when he went back to try and rescue his men still in the blazing aircraft that he was shot and killed by a stray German bullet.

Earlier in 1942 the 8th Army had attended a memorial service at Cairo Cathedral during which General Jock Campbell was presented with his Victoria Cross for inspirational leadership at Sidi Rezegh. He then took command of the 7th Armoured Division and General Gott took command of 13 Corps. Two weeks after receiving his VC Jock Campbell was killed in a car crash. Thirteen is not considered to be the luckiest of numbers. The loss of General Jock Campbell was a serious blow to the 8th Army. The loss of General Gott was devastating. He was born in August 1897, on the 13th.

Who would take over now?

The startling news of Gott's death possibly revived Rommel's spirits.

On finding himself ambushed at Alamein he knew that there must be a weakness in the Alamein Line minefields through which the British southern prong would move to encircle the Germans.

In late June his surveyors had discovered that the 'gap' was at the Ruweisal Ridge. Rommel had attacked, but this 'gap' had been under constant watch by Gott's Armoured Division, and the Germans were driven back to the limited confines in front of the Alamein Line.

Rommel took sick leave in September, and again at the beginning of October, leaving the fate of his Afrika Korps to his fellow senior officers.

Perhaps his reverse at Reweisal Ridge had shown him that it would be impossible for him to break through and he had 'thrown in the towel'. Why else would he spend so long in Germany? Soldiers might say that by his prolonged 'sick leave' in Germany he was 'swinging the lead'.

Gott was dead. His men had repulsed the Germans. This thought must have haunted Rommel. It is surely unfair that General Gott should become the forgotten man of the Western Desert. What must his family have thought when the fame of Alamein went to another man? The future had held so much for Strafer Gott . . . and within twenty four hours of his appointment to highest office . . . a stray German bullet took it all away. He must not be forgotten.

Can we, therefore, compose, a posthumous headline to honour General Gott?, something like:-

GOTT'S GHOST ROUTS ROMMEL!

MASSACRE AT ALAMEIN?

512 R.E. Survey Detachment to South African Air Survey Unit, Maadi, Summer 1942

Coxon, Rogers, Tubby Newland, Booth, Titheridge, Bob Leach, Brooks, Powell, Doc Watson, Dan Godley, Russell (kneeling) Ira Peace, Gordon Lavarack, Geoff Saunders

CHAPTER NINE

Churchill's Desert Dilemma

Churchill had things to contemplate other than the Desert War after General Gott had been appointed Auchinleck's successor.

There had been anti-Churchill murmurs in certain parts of Britain by people not satisfied with the way the war was going, but the Government had backed Churchill's leadership. He had the support of the Labour Party and the Trade Unions. Britain was more united in leadership than ever before. There was no reasonable alternative to Churchill remaining as Prime Minister.

But Churchill knew his grand speeches would not sustain the country forever.

'Arm yourselves and be men of valour!' was all very inspiring and effective. He had, however, claimed too many 'turning points' in the war. Really there should only be one turning point in the battle against Hitler's evil regime.

'We will wage war against a monstrous tyranny!'

Victory! Victory at all costs. No panic. No surrender until *'the curse of Hitler is lifted from the brows of men!'*.

The saving of the bulk of our Army in the evacuation from Dunkirk had been a 'turning point' in our favour.

Winning the Battle of Britain in the air had been a 'turning point' in the war.

Japan bringing America into the war had been a 'turning point' and so had Germany's invasion of Russia. Victory at Alamein would be at least the fifth 'turning point' in Britain's favour.

This 'turning point' theme had been overdone and Churchill knew that he needed something more solid to offer the British people. There was no doubt in Churchill's mind that the most secure thing he could offer would be a confirmed alliance and commitment by Roosevelt and Stalin to form an effective and workable triumvirate. The British had had no support since France had fallen, but with such powerful allies as Russia and America surely the British people would see that Hitler could have no chance of defeating such a dream team.

Churchill would have to woo Roosevelt and Stalin, and to do this he had to meet them face to face as often as possible.

Roosevelt had not wanted to enter the war and this was not surprising when we bear in mind that he was considered to be an isolationist. Indeed, America was jealous of Britain having such a vast Empire and was in no mood to sacrifice American blood to sustain Britain's hold on such a large area of the globe.

History has told us how Churchill visited America and how his speeches at the President's home, The White House, won the Americans over, *'If my mother had been English and my father American instead of the other way round I might have got here on my own!'* was a very impressive use of humour.

We know that he then went to Canada where the French influence was far from friendly. The 1940 Government in France, certain that Britain would fall, had stated that Britain was like a chicken with the noose already round its neck. The RAF had beaten off Hitler's expected victory and Churchill in making reference to the French comment brought the Canadian Assembly to a riot of laughter with his comment, beautifully timed. *'Some chicken, some neck!'*

(It is hardly necessary to remind ourselves that this wisecrack was turned into a popular song.)

Roosevelt and Churchill became close friends and as a result America sent weapons and Britain sent supplies to Russia. Mrs Churchill gave support with her 'Aid to Russia' campaign.

Despite lack of enthusiasm for war by senior American officers

Churchill and Roosevelt became 'great buddies'.

The next capture in the Churchill net had to be Stalin, so a meeting in Moscow was arranged.

In terms of lives being lost Russia was bearing the brunt of Germany's aggression. Allied promises had been made to Stalin and these had not been kept. There was a frosty atmosphere when Churchill met Stalin. Humour would not see the British Prime Minister through this time. Stalin was on the attack. He had been promised an Anglo-American invasion before the end of 1942. Was Churchill going to honour this? *'You British are afraid of fighting. The Germans and Russians are not afraid to die in large numbers!'*

Stalin showed no appreciation for the equipment Britain had sent to him via the dangerous North Atlantic run.

'If you fought the Germans fiercely you would not be afraid of them!' Stalin sneered. He spoke as if he believed that the number of dead, represented the strength of national sacrifice.

Humour would fail here so Churchill decided to try anger. He knew the room in his Russian hotel would be bugged and that his telegrams would be read. Good. He sent a telegram to Deputy Prime Minister Clement Attlee telling him how rude and ungrateful Stalin was. To those with him in his room he raged against Stalin knowing this was being bugged and translated and shown to Stalin.

Stalin *was* impressed. Churchill *was* a man and not a weed.

Stalin then accepted Churchill's reasons for delay and prudence, and a great banquet was held in Moscow in Churchill's honour. The Alliance held, and Churchill now was in tune with both Roosevelt and Stalin.

Then suddenly, and certainly 'out of the blue', came the news that Gott had been killed.

Was Fate taking a hand?

Was this an opportunity for Churchill to re-think his desert campaign so that America could be involved and Russia satisfied?

There were many 'desert experts' out there, any one of whom would carry out the 'Auchinleck Blueprint', but, would any one of them wait until details with the Americans were confirmed? It was very unlikely. These Desert Rats stuck together. Churchill had already given Auchinleck the sack for waiting until September 9th or thereabouts. It would be October or November before the Americans could be in place in western North Africa. Well, what about someone from England? Churchill invariably found himself on a different wavelength from the desert warriors. English-based officers were more to his liking. It might serve his purpose better to have someone from home soil.

There was Major-General Hobart ('Hobo' to his men, who adored him) who had been dismissed from the desert despite his obvious skill and loyal following. He had been a close friend of Strafer Gott. The trouble had been caused by jealousy and a conflict of personalities. Hobart had been at loggerheads with fellow desert General 'Jumbo' Maitland-Wilson who as a consequence had wanted 'Hobo' removed as Commander of the 7th Armoured Division, and Wavell had agreed. Hobart's men had been shocked and showed their feelings by cheering him to the echo as he left, making obvious their preference for him rather than Maitland-Wilson. One general had to go and Wavell could see that even the desert was not large enough for the two men. At the time Gott had wanted Hobert to fight Wavell's order, but Major-General O'Moore Creagh took Hobo's place and that was the end of the matter. Auchinleck later banished Maitland-Wilson to 9th Army in Beirut. The desert was not the place for quarrels.

Hobart? Churchill now thought carefully. Would Hobart agree to a delay until the Americans landed in Tripoli later in 1942? Churchill doubted it. Hobart had become 'man of the desert' and would not take part in a lie, no matter how important Churchill considered it for the war effort in general.

Hobart's sister Betty had married a fellow by the name of Bernard Montgomery. Spiky little character. Making a big noise in South East England Command. Will of his own. Son of a bishop. Not too popular but that didn't seem to bother him.

A call to the War Office on August 7th confirmed that Montgomery was in Scotland and had been picked to command the Northern Task Force of OPERATION TORCH, the secretly planned Anglo-American invasion of North Africa. (The rumour was that South East Command, England, were glad to get rid of him and 'promotion' to the desert would achieve that. A later theory was that he was the only one cocky enough to handle the patronisingly confident Americans, who were to include the notorious General Patton!).

Any Middle East experience? Churchill began to check and there was much in Montgomery's 'file' that suited Churchill's new plans for the desert.

Was the fellow married. He had married a widow, Betty Carver.

Betty Carver's husband had been a sapper, killed at Gallipoli in 1915 and leaving Betty with two sons. She met Bernard Montgomery in Lenk, Switzerland, under strange circumstances in 1926. It seems that the previous year Montgomery, at the age of 38, finally fell under Cupid's arrow for a seventeen-year-old beauty called Betty Anderson. He met her at Dinard, Brittany, and courted her vigorously by drawing battle formations in the sand to impress his loved one with his military skill. Betty's father was in the Indian Army but, despite this military background, she wanted more romantic things than imaginary battle scenes scratched by her suitor in the warm sands of Brittany.

Montgomery proposed to Betty Anderson but she turned him down. (She eventually married a sugar planter in India, in 1930).

However, Betty was to meet Montgomery again, in 1926 at Lenk in Switzerland. In her party was a widow, Betty Carver, the same age group as Montgomery so the first Betty introduced the second Betty to Montgomery.

There was now another swift change in the Montgomery life style. He no longer wished to opt for a life of celibacy and he seemed all too ready to give up his bachelor life, and never mind about it being to the detriment of his military career! He wasted no time in courting his second Betty and having learned something from his failure as a suitor in the sands of Northern France he refrained from drawing battle plans in the snow of Switzerland and became excited when he saw that he was making progress with Betty Mark 2.

He got on well with her two sons.

Not many months had passed when Betty, realising where the relationship was heading, said, "I don't think we ought to see each other again."

Montgomery got it right this time.

"Don't be silly. I love you!"

Betty Carver, nee Hobart, burst into tears, and they were married in the summer of 1927. At the time Montgomery was at the Staff College at Camberley (where he remained until 1929).

The wedding was a bit of a Spartan affair. Montgomery did not have a 'Stag Night' celebration before the wedding, instead he and Betty dined at the Junior United Service Club in King Charles Street, London. His father, the bishop, assisted by son Colin Roger (now a curate), conducted the wedding ceremony. Brian Montgomery was best man, and Betty's brother 'Hobo' gave her away. The two stepsons, John and Dick Carver were present. There was no reception or wedding party. Immediately after the ceremony Montgomery and Betty left for their honeymoon, in Switzerland.

It turned out to be a good marriage. Betty was about the same age as Montgomery (39). She was always laughing and was cheerful. In appearance she was dark and vivacious, not exactly pretty but extremely charming. She simply laughed at Montgomery's eccentricities and they became a devoted couple. They lived in Chiswick Mall, not far from the Montgomery's family home in Chiswick. She was a cultured lady, her friends including A. P. Herbert and Dick Shepherd.

Among the students at the Staff College were several who were to gain distinction in the Desert War: Dorman-Smith, C. W. M. Norrie, and 'Gertie' Tuker the future leader of the 4th Indian Division.

Bernard and Betty Montgomery had a son, 18th August 1928, and he was christened David. They lived in a bungalow-type house in the married quarters of the Staff College.

This all seems very normal (except for the mean streak in his wedding arrangements), until one reads a certain account written by one of Montgomery's brothers, Brian, about a family reunion in 1933. Montgomery and Betty were on leave from Alexandria and when the time to go (from the family's second home, *New Park*, in Molville, Co. Donegal, Ireland) arrived Montgomery's mother remarked that Bernard and Betty would be *'staying in London before flying back to Egypt so that Betty can get some clothes!'*

It was a reasonable assumption because Betty and Bernard were due to leave Alexandria for posting to India and new clothes would be very much in order for an officer's lady arriving in a strange continent. It would also be nice to visit a theatre, Mrs Montgomery senior thought.

His mother had brought up nine children (six boys and three girls) and performed with distinction her duties as the wife of a bishop. She fully expected her son to offer his wife the luxury of a few days in London.

But Bernard would have none of it.

'Certainly not. All she needs, all any woman needs, is one serviceable dress and a waterproof hat!'

Churchill might have smiled at that. Maybe the pig-headed Montgomery was the man he was looking for. What was his educational background?

St Pauls School, held back for a couple of terms either because he was lazy or because he lacked academic ability. Nickname, 'Monkey'. Best thing his teachers could say was that 'he was good at games'. Severe telling-off by his autocratic mother and his work improved during his extra two terms at school.

Military Training?

Not very good. He entered Sandhurst in January 1907, above average age because of being held back at school. At the Entrance Examination he was 72nd out of 170 accepted. On becoming a lance corporal he became leader of a rough gang who terrorised the younger gentleman cadets. (He was already 'pulling rank' by making unfair use of his single stripe). For one ugly cruel and criminal offence he was reduced to the ranks and his suitability for fitness to ever hold a commission came under review. The terrible incident concerned Montgomery and his gang of six picking on a cadet who was in the process of changing into his blue Mess Uniform. He was wearing underpants and shirt. While Montgomery's gang of six pinioned the cadet's arms and legs so that he could not move Montgomery set fire to the cadet's shirt tails. The youngster was in terrible agony (he required prolonged hospital treatment) and it looked as though Montgomery's military career was over.

However, with a mother who is the wife of a bishop, who is 43 years old, still very attractive, completely autocratic, Montgomery had privileged support. Maud Montgomery was going to save her son at all costs. No Montgomery must be dismissed from Sandhurst. The ghosts of the Military Montgomeries would turn in their graves. Lady Montgomery invited the commandant at Sandhurst to her home for the weekend. In those days a bishop, and the wife of a Bishop, held great sway and influence. The colonel (I/C Sandhurst) was persuaded to give Montgomery one more chance and the punishment was restricted to having to stay on at Sandhurst for an extra six months. This would delay the date of his commission and affect his seniority.

It was a family tradition that the Montgomeries entered the Indian Army. The pay was better because their service was usually in the Far East, and promotion was easier: captain after nine years, major after a few more, and so on. In British Service promotion was governed by vacancies arising, thus a subaltern could remain so for as long as twenty years. Despite Montgomery's extra six months he did not pass high enough to be eligible for the Indian Army, and this was a great disappointment to him and to his parents. He left Sandhurst in July 1908. He was reported as being 'good at games'. Not a particularly inspiring recommendation. He was certainly not a scholar.

In 1908 he was posted to 1st Battalion Royal Warwickshire Regiment stationed in India. He took no part in the social life there. In his *Memoirs* Montgomery confirms that he had a very poor opinion of the efficiency of his fellow officers. He was 5' 8½" and perhaps the physical effort of having to 'look up to' taller men prompted his belittling indictment of his comrades.

Not knowing what else to make of him the C/O nominated him battalion sports officer, 1911, but Montgomery was to show that although he might be 'good at games' he was far from being 'a good sportsman'.

The German battleship *Gneisenau* was on a courtesy visit to India and Montgomery was given **strict instructions** to pick a football team balanced to give the German sailors a fair game. (Hardly necessary to any other sports officer, but it was known what a little so-and-so Montgomery was). It was an important diplomatic and social visit with everyone on their most polite behaviour. In all sports there are balancing methods: boxers must be the same weight, race horses carry handicapping weights so each has a chance of winning, golfers have handicaps, an equal chance is what sport is all about. The sailors from the *Gneisenau* had been at sea and hardly had time to find their land legs. Anyone but Montgomery would have had the decency to field a weakened team to allow the German sailors to give a fair account of themselves and thus have a chance of giving the spectators a good game to watch. Not so Montgomery.

To the acute embarrassment of everyone he fielded his strongest team and beat the Germans 40-Nil. Can you imagine that? A goal every couple of minutes! It must have been like some cruel joke, like the burnt shirt-tails at Sandhurst.

Servicemen do not mince their words and at having to watch this disgraceful massacre instead of a balanced match we can imagine the comments of the squaddies! This might have been said;

"Bloody 'ell! This is not a game. Who picked this f...ing team?"

"Lieutenant Montgomery."

"Oh, that little s... house!"

Others might have said, "Good old Montgomery!"

His classmates at St Paul's held views on 'Monkey' Montgomery's idea of sportsmanship. In a mock school report they wrote: *The Monkey... makes its nest in football fields... pulls out the hairs of neighbouring animals, this it calls 'tackling'. Shows no mercy... stamps on heads... many other inconceivable atrocities... no doubt to prove its patriotism.*

An infinite capacity for inflicting pain on others?

Or a schoolboy prankster?

When World War One arrived Montgomery was in Ireland, age 26 and with the rank of lieutenant. By 1915 he had been promoted to brigade major. During the war he saw the awful slaughter at Ypres and Passchendaele which cost Britain 240,000 casualties. At the end of the war he was a lieutenant-general, GSO of the 47th Infantry Division. His first independent command was O/C 17th Battalion Royal Fusiliers, based near Cologne. In 1920 he was sent to the Staff College at Camberley where the director of staff declared him to be 'a bloody menace'.

In 1921 he was a brigade-major with the 17th Infantry in Cork, Ireland. The IRA were very active and Montgomery wrote to his father, *"... anyone who interferes with any officer or soldier is* **shot at once!**"

(In 1969 a cousin, Lt.-Col Hugh Montgomery, was shot by the IRA).

MASSACRE AT ALAMEIN?

In 1922 Montgomery was in Plymouth, in 1923 in York where he made friends with Lieutenant de Guingand who was to play a part in the run-up to Alamein in 1942. By 1927 Montgomery was a Lt-Colonel. In 1931 he went as O/C 1st Battalion of his regiment, 1st Royal Warwickshire, and was based in Palestine. Betty joined her husband in Jerusalem. Then he and Betty served in India, returning as brigadier O/C 9th Infantry Division at Portsmouth. It was 1937 and on October 19th Betty died, leaving her son David who was 9 years old. (David was looked after by Major and Mrs Reynolds at Hindhead, Surrey).

Montgomery 're-married his profession' and Betty's calming influence no longer soothed his inflated ego.

In 1938 he was in dire trouble with the War Office for leasing Government land to a circus promoter to raise funds. War was approaching and his senior commander, General Wavell, allowed the affair to drag on until it was forgotten in the more serious preparations for war against Hitler.

Montgomery was sent to Palestine in 1938. This, his second visit there, was of course without Betty's company and Montgomery was not feeling too cheerful. On Montgomery's first day his number two had reported that several Arabs had been killed while the British quelled a public disturbance. The number two was nervous. Would this new man, Montgomery, sanction the killing of Arabs to maintain law and order? He need not have worried, Montgomery's reported reply was, *"Have you killed enough Arabs to keep the area quiet?"* and that summed up his attitude to the Palestine problem. Not for Montgomery to look into Arab fears of Zionist expansion. No seeking a fair interpretation of the Balfour Declaration, giving one third of Palestine to the Jews. No seeking to understand the Arabs as Lawrence of Arabia and many others with human instincts of fair play had done.

"Have you killed enough Arabs to keep the area quiet?" That is what seemed to matter most to Montgomery. Or was he too lonely to think further?

Back in England in August 1939 Montgomery took command of the 3rd Infantry Division and trained his men hard. In November he was again in trouble with Higher Authority because of an order he had issued concerning venereal disease. This was not the first time he had given his men sex instruction. In Alexandria he had given some offence with his advice on sex. He now referred to sex as 'horizontal refreshment' and urged his men to ask for *Capote Anglaise* when entering a chemist shop, and drop the term *French Letter*. (Why should these damned foreigners have a monopoly on sex!).

He also told his men to attend the Early Treatment (ET) centres if they became infected with VD. *If you do not know where the nearest ET Unit is, ask a policeman.*

For a chap like Montgomery to give advice on sex is quite hilarious and an unknown lyricist in the Royal Signals 'took the Mickey' in poetic style;

The General was worried and very ill at ease,
He was haunted by the subject of venereal disease,
. . . . .
The Adjutants explained that 'capote' did not mean cup
And 'refreshment horizontal' must be taken standing up,
. . . . .
Now the General is happy and perfectly at ease,
No longer is he troubled with venereal disease.

(Cupid. R. Sig.)

This interference in medical matters by Montgomery was taken very seriously by his superiors and his command was in jeopardy yet again. Montgomery was saved by General Alan Brooke who realised that there was a war on and more pressing matters took precedence. Montgomery was sent to France and after Dunkirk he resumed command of his 3rd Infantry Division. He met General Auchinleck who was O/C Southern Command and the two men did not get on, Montgomery causing another unnecessary upset. Auchinleck had ordered all troops to keep their arms 'nearby and handy', an innocuous enough order, but Montgomery told his men to disobey it. There was a terrible furore, of course, but the quarrel died down when Auchinleck went to India as C-in-C. (The two men were to meet again in 1942, as we shall see in the next chapter).

In 1940/41 Montgomery was GOC South East Army, and he lectured that it was an essential element of leadership to engage in self-publicity. His seniors responded by stating that real leaders did not need 'self-publicity'. Montgomery loved to hold the stage, and his brother Brian said that this came from their mother. She, too, loved to hold the stage. Auchinleck had no difficulty in attracting loyalty, neither did Wavell nor most of the other great leaders. But, they had 'presence' and eschewed all 'self-publicity'.

Churchill noted that Montgomery, commanding in South East England, had placed certain very unpopular marriage restrictions on his men during their strict training. (He'd lost his wife so why should his men have . . . ! It would be better for them to get out of their cold beds and engage in early-morning Swedish Drill).

Lt.-Colonel Walter Rowley, OBE, novelist (*48-Hour Pass . . . Hong Kong*) speaking conversationally about when he was first commissioned and reported to South East Command when Montgomery was O/C told his friends that this small man came bustling in. On the wall was a map of the South of England and Northern France. Montgomery smacked the English portion of the map with his cane, saying in a loud voice, "We ah Har!". He slapped the North of France, "And the enemy ah thar!". Another slap of the cane, "They could invade us har!, or, har!"

Montgomery's affected speech was possibly due more to his mother than to any public school influence. Bishop Montgomery was sent to Tasmania and his children spent several years there during which time their mother insisted that they did not pick up the Tasmanian accent but spoke 'good' English and she would correct their accent when necessary. Anything other than 'good' English was 'common'. Bernard, ever eager to attract attention, probably overdid the 'public school' voice when he was in Tasmania. Also, there is no doubt that in the 1920s and 1930s the 'public school' voice or, as some people named it, 'the BBC voice', did command respect and obedience. Most leaders held attention though, by using a polite, modulated but cultured voice. By the 1940s people were less impressed by the snobbish 'affected' voice and thus Montgomery's voice sounded pretentious and Walter Rowley was one of many who remembered it with a certain lack of respect, albeit with some amusement. It was the kind of voice music hall comedians would use impersonating a 'toff'.

MASSACRE AT ALAMEIN?

First impressions did not flatter Montgomery. David Stirling remembered him as 'quite a short man, not fully grown, an underweight fighting bantam cock'. Regular soldier RSM McMasters, of the Hussars, described Montgomery as 'a short wiry fellow, with a bee in his bonnet about PT.'

Montgomery was 'good at games' but he was not master of any particular sport. He seemed to have no cultural depth or artistic talent like, for example, Churchill and his painting, Wavell and his poetry, and Auchinleck with his linguistic abilities. Neither was he renowned for, say, skill at Bridge or Chess.

Despite having the free use of horses while in Tasmania he was never able to properly control a horse, as officers were supposed to. His brother Brian tells a 'horse' story about his brother. On parade in India Montgomery, on horseback, was berated by the inspecting officer for being six paces out of centre. Any other officer would have moved his horse six paces, but Montgomery ordered the whole of his battalion "Six paces to the right . . . March!" Was he showing that 'he was in place and everyone else was out of order, so everyone else had to move', or, was he showing his inability to control his own horse? (Brian Montgomery, in telling this story, confesses that it might be apocryphal but it is at least typical).

Churchill knew one thing, South East Command would make no protest wherever Montgomery was moved.

The Prime Minister probably believed he would have no difficulty in manipulating a man like Montgomery. A little bit of flattery. Churchill may have thought along these lines.

"Look here, General Montgomery. I want this desert business cleared up. Wavell took his men to Benghazi and then brought them back into Egypt. Auchinleck, and I believe you do not share his opinion on military matters, took his men to Benghazi, and back. The men must be demoralised. I need someone like you to pep them up. I will send you all the equipment you need, especially new and strong American tanks. Don't strike until I give the command. Take your time. Build up the men's morale, build up your supplies. Beat this man Rommel. The Germans have made him a national hero. You can beat him. And I can make you a national hero. Take your men to Benghazi, but do not bring them back to Alamein, take them on to Tripoli. All the way this time. Show Stalin we can win a real battle, at Alamein. And, this is between you and me, I am hoping to bring in the Americans in North Africa. The Middle East generals do not know this. Tell only Auchinleck, in strict secrecy, that I might be able to link up with the Americans. I do not want Auchinleck complaining or criticising in public our delay. Tell no one else because nothing is finalised yet. Do you know, Stalin told me that we British are afraid of the Germans. He thinks we do not know how to fight, or how to die in large numbers. He is losing millions in Russia while we pussyfoot around. We might open a second front, not in France, but up through the soft underbelly of Italy. I need a little more time. Are you with me? Do you understand?"

Whatever Churchill might have said was thwarted because Montgomery was still in Scotland. So, on August 8th 1942 the War Office telephoned Montgomery cancelling his trip to the western coastline of North Africa and ordering him to report to London and pick up instructions for a new posting.

The full details of the instructions are not fully known but they were sufficiently exciting for the fiery little general to get to Cairo as quickly as possible and seek the ordered private meeting with Auchinleck.

Then with unseemly speed he took himself to Alamein where he set up his HQ in a caravan **forty eight hours before he should have done!**

There were those who thought this was a bit of a snub to Auchinleck, and to Alexander who was still senior to Montgomery in the Middle East Command.

CHAPTER TEN

Montgomery in Egypt

Montgomery's arrival in Egypt can be likened in several respects to that of his brother Colin Roger Montgomery's arrival at my parish church circa 1930.

The latter's arrival at St John's Church, Egremont, Wallasey, Cheshire is described in a 1992 article I wrote in response to one written earlier that year by that eminent historian and lecturer on military matters, Barrie Pitt (Books: *The Crucible of War, Zeebrugge, Coronel and Falkland, The Battle of the Atlantic, et al*) in our Savage Club magazine, 'Drumbeat'.

Barrie Pitt had written the article describing a meeting with fellow Brother Savage Bernard Montgomery, **Monty**, and Barrie's opening sentence recorded Montgomery's fraternal greeting, *" 'Ah! I see you're a member of my Club' said the Field Marshal, pointing at my tie."*

It was the final paragraph with its iconoclastic opening phrase which particularly attracted my attention; *" 'Cocky little bugger, isn't he?' remarked a corporal nearby"*, and this prompted me to pen a reply, **Monty's Brother**.

The contents of Barrie's article and its demolitionary ending reminded me very strongly of Montgomery's brother, our vicar, Colin Roger.

Another brother, Brian, has written that hereditary instincts came to the fore in their family so it is not really surprising that Colin Roger's arrival to take over our parish was very similar in behaviour pattern to Bernard's arrival in the desert to take over at Alamein. The similarities are very revealing.

I reproduce my article on Montgomery's brother and use it as a template to explain Montgomery's immediate actions and behaviour on arrival in the desert.

Monty's Brother. © Bob Leach 1992.

I was interested in Barrie Pitt's excellent article, Monty, *(Drumbeat 44), for a number of reasons, one of them being that I knew Monty's brother, Colin Roger Montgomery.*

It was not a happy relationship.

If you bear in mind that I was born in 1917 and that the first World Scout Jamboree was held in 1928, you will see that my attendance at the famous camp was the year I changed my status from cub to scout. A very impressionable age, one each person remembers well. The World Jamboree (known as the 'Mudboree' because of the incessant rain) was held at nearby Arrowe Park, Birkenhead. Wallasey is on the other side of Birkenhead docks, on the south bank of the Mersey. Liverpool is on the opposite bank. Our scout troop, being so near to the famous camp site, used it regularly during the 1930s for weekend camps. This troop I belonged to was The Ninth Wallasey, and in brackets underneath the name-tag (we wore one on each shoulder) was 'St John's Own'.

The vicar of St John's, the mother church of our scout troop, was a kindly old gentleman known respectfully as 'Doctor Bond'.

The nicknames given to other leaders in those peaceful days give evidence of the social gentility of that era; the curate was *Mr Woodcock, 'Timberdick', the scoutmaster Steve Saville was known by his favourite sweets, 'Butterballs', (you see what I mean about those genteel days of prewar innocence. Who today could carry with sang froid a nickname like that!), and the assistant scoutmaster was universally known as 'Golly' Wilson (and there were no racial overtones relating to Golly or the marmalade Gollywog. Indeed, 'Nigger Brown' was a favourite colour for ladies' skirts and jumpers,

---

*Drowned during the war en route to South Africa.

MASSACRE AT ALAMEIN?

and my school friend Nigel Ward was forever known as 'Nigger' Ward, even to present times, 1990s.)

As I type this article I have on my desk a faded cutting from a wartime copy of The Wallasey News.

"Honour for Wallasey Scoutmaster. It is with great pleasure that I announce that Mr J. H. Wilson ("Golly") of the 9th Wallasey Group, has been mentioned in Dispatches in the recent birthday honours list. Mr Wilson is serving in the Navy and is at present in a naval hospital where he has been for the last three months. I got nothing out of 'Golly' as to what the award was for but hope to tell you in these notes at a later date."

Those of pre-war vintage will, from the above, be able to appreciate the very amiable relationship between the 9th Wallasey Boy Scouts and St John's Church.

Then the much-loved Dr Bond retired.

The new vicar was Colin Roger Montgomery.

Our quiet, peaceful church was turned into a nightmare of chaos, change, anger, resignations, and so on. I was too young to be part of it. I simply remember the chaos, the disintegration of the long-established societies within the church, the pain and the fury, and could only watch as the 'St John's Own' was removed from our shoulder tags when Butterballs and Colin Roger finally parted company.

It all began over church parades and weekend camps.

There were many church parades in those days. Apart from Saints' Days, we had Mayor's Parade, Empire Parade, Armistice Parade, and so on, and they were usually held in the months from September to April. The spring and summer months were given over to weekend camps and the annual fortnight's camp during the school summer holiday.

Colin Roger asked Butterballs how many church parades the Scouts did, and he said about twelve a year.

"Once a month!" Colin Roger is supposed to have replied and, when May and June came he wanted his monthly church parade. Butterballs and Golly expected a reasonable acceptance by Colin

MASSACRE AT ALAMEIN?

Roger when it was explained that weekend camps at Arrowe Park meant that church parades were confined to the autumn and winter months. To their astonishment Colin Roger would have none of it and, to cut a long story short, it finally became a case of, 'if you fail to parade during June, July and August then you cannot have the use of the church hall'. Of course, it was not as blatant and as final as that at the beginning. The tensions grew. I am just reporting what happened after much unpleasant business between scout-master and vicar.

So, Butterballs and Golly told Colin Roger we could manage without his church hall, and three rooms above a shop were rented and the scouts moved in there.

On Saturday nights a whist-drive was held in these new headquarters and we heard that we scouts were not the only ones upset by the new vicar.

For example:

"Mrs Thomson has held her sewing class on Tuesday evenings for the last thirty years and Colin Roger (everyone seemed to use this form of identification for the vicar) wants her to move to Saturday morning."

"It's ridiculous, and I don't blame Mrs Thomson for holding her class at her own home. How can she expect her class to move to Saturday morning."

Other activities were spreading their wings. Many of the local football teams were affiliated to churches and bore their name; 'New Brighton Baptists', 'Saint Mary's', 'Saint Hilary's', 'Seacombe Presbyterian', and it soon became noticeable that some of St John's best players were with other teams. Those remaining joined with some of the scouts and I became secretary of 'Central United', so-called because we played in Central Park. I wrote the match reports, and some years ago I was researching at the Newspaper Museum at Collingwood, north London, and when I finished I amused myself by looking up some of these reports I'd written half a century ago for The Wallasey News.

My little crowd and I left Colin Roger's church and moved down *the road to the Congregational Church. This was because we no longer felt easy doing our homework on the back pew during the Sunday Evensong service. Under Dr Bond there had been no danger. Had he spotted what we were doing he would probably have come and helped us. But this Colin Roger! Oh no . . . he would have given the game away had he discovered that we were swotting and not praying. We feared that this pale-eyed, thin-lipped autocrat would snitch on us to either our parents or our headmaster . . . or both! Things were much more easy-going at the Congregational Church and the Reverend Ian Darke made us feel very welcome, homework on the back pew an' all!*

Another departure under Colin Roger seemed to be among the tenors and basses in the choir, and this corresponded with an increase in the number of choirboys. I had two young brothers, Jim and Philip who was the youngest. Philip sang in St John's choir and, from one practice a week, he began to attend on two evenings a week. Colin Roger was making the boys' choir into a sort of club, maybe to offset the loss of the scouts. There was definitely competition because, in the summer, my brother Jim and I attended summer camp with the scouts, while Philip went to Ireland for two weeks with Colin Roger and his choirboys. They stayed at a *large house, with beds and taps with hot water and other comparative luxuries. We scouts had to forage for wood and water, and dig our own latrines, and live the outdoor life as set out by Baden Powell.

One idea Colin Roger had for his choir was the appointment of a 'Boy Bishop', and for one year the appointed boy had to go through all the ceremonial of a bishop. Did our parish priest have personal ambitions to become a bishop? (After the war he did, but I was told it was in South Africa. Perhaps the Archbishop of Canterbury feared that Colin Roger was after his job!) Colin Roger was a great one for ceremonial and I remember the fuss and bother at his inauguration at Saint John's. It seemed to go on and on. There were marches round the church with robed bodies carrying shepherd's crooks and others swinging pots of smoking incense, and incessant stopping and

MASSACRE AT ALAMEIN?

starting. The congregation did not know what had hit it! Dr Bond had been very moderate on ceremonial.

On looking up my football reports of the early 1930s it was noticeable that Colin Roger Montgomery seemed to get his name in the local paper as frequently as Central United football club.

Wallasey was alive with parish priests, but it was Colin Roger who managed to think up something every week to gain publicity. One thing he let be known was that he had a brother, Bernard Montgomery, who was an Army officer. On top of that, Colin Roger made sure we knew that he was not only our vicar at St John's but also chaplain to the Army.

"Aye," said one of a trio of men sipping tea during the interval at our boy scout's whist drive, "one kills 'em and the other buries 'em!"

"It were better under Dr Bond. This one shows off too much." and so to my paraphrase of Barrie Pitt's last paragraph;

"Cocky little bugger, isn't he?" said the third man in the group, and those are the same words Barrie Pitt used to begin his final paragraph of his Drumbeat *article. Can we say that any similarity between the two brothers is more than mere coincidence?*

Colin Roger Montgomery edged out the scouts and eased in his own boy's club from his choir boys.

Bernard Montgomery edged out the Desert Generals and eased in Generals straight from England.

Colin Roger's action divided families. In my family, my two younger brothers were faced with divided loyalties, Jim going to camp with the scouts and Philip going to *New Park, the Montgomery's 18th century quarry stone slate roofed ten bedroom home in Moville, Ireland.

Bernard Montgomery's action divided the 8th Army. New arrivals from Britain taunted the Desert Rats with names such as 'Cairo Canaries' and 'Groppi's Light Infantry' and the seasoned Men of the Desert replied with scornful cries of, "Get your knees brown!"

*The house, New Park, was sold in 1949 and became a hotel. The family also had a home in Chiswick.

Colin Roger brought friction to St John's Church and Bernard brought friction to the Desert.

The first brother had new leaders for his boy's club and the second brought new leaders from Britain, Lt.-General Oliver Leese and Lt.-General Brian Horrocks, for his Desert Army at Alamein.

Brian Horrocks arrived on August 19th straight from commanding the 9th Armoured Division in Northumberland and it is difficult to imagine a greater contrast. He was given command of 13 Corps. Horrocks admits that the Desert Rats and their leaders had become 'an exclusive club'. These desert veterans were unlikely to welcome a new, unknown leader who had no desert experience. To have 'white knees' was an unforgiveable sin in the desert. According to the Montgomery philosophy the sooner this 'exclusive club' was broken up the better for his personal ego. He was afraid of anyone who had more experience of the desert than he himself, hence, the appointment of a man from Northumberland! Twenty-five years after the Battle of Alamein Sir Brian Horrocks admitted in a Sunday newspaper that Montgomery was wrong to imply, as he did in his sneaky manner, that the morale of the original 8th Army was poor. Montgomery's orders to Horrocks were significant, 'Hold your line but don't lose too many men because **it will interfere with my main plan to drive the Axis Forces out of Egypt!**' HIS plan! What did he imagine Auchinleck and Gott planned?

This is the rotten bit; Montgomery told Horrocks and others, "I don't want any further withdrawals", implying that Auchinleck had planned a withdrawal. Let us study how Montgomery stage-managed his impression of Auchinleck's weakness as against Montgomery's firmness.

The first thing he did on landing in Egypt (after having breakfast at Mena House Hotel) was to hold a secret meeting with Auchinleck in which no one else was present. What went on between the two men was based on what Churchill had said to the War Office when he appointed Montgomery. It was natural that neither Churchill nor the War Ofice wanted Auchinleck reminding people that he had been given the sack for delaying the Battle of Alamein yet the man taking over had been instructed to delay the battle even longer than the date Auchinleck had decided upon, i.e., on or about September 9th.

Auchinleck must had been told that the influence of Stalin and the co-operation of Roosevelt were matters which were requiring a change of plan. There is also no doubt that Montgomery and Auchinleck had a gentleman's agreement to accept the plan and say nothing to create a hiatus at GHQ.

Sadly, however, it was not in the character of Bernard Montgomery, or Colin Roger, to miss a chance of gaining the upper hand at the expense of others.

Colin Roger's treatment of the scoutmaster can be likened to Bernard's distastefully offhand treatment of Auchinleck.

The scoutmaster in saying that there were about twelve church parades a year did not say that they were strictly one per month. That was the vicar's interpretation and one that suited him because it gave him the opportunity to use this twisted interpretation to discredit the scoutmaster.

Auchinleck was asked by Montgomery about his plan of attack and also about contingency plans in case of withdrawal. There had been no doubt in Auchinleck's mind that if the conditions did not change then there was no way he could lose the Battle of Alamein. Contingency plans were necessary, however, just in case conditions did change. For example, at one time Churchill feared that Russia would capitulate. This would have set free millions of Germans. (A recent television programme claimed that five million Germans died on Russian soil. This shows the immensity of the Russian campaign). If that had happened Hitler might have possibly decided to use his troops no longer required in Russia to bolster up his Afrika Korps and it was only prudent of Auchinleck to have a withdrawal plan worked out 'just in case'. It was normal military strategy. It was common sense.

Montgomery, however, never talked of Auchinleck's plan of attack but superciliously never missed an opportunity to declare that 'he would never retreat to the Delta!' Sir Brian Horrocks admits that in his initial briefing Montgomery told him, 'there will be no further withdrawal' which, by implication, suggested that had Auchinleck still been in charge there would have been a withdrawal.

Brian Montgomery is quite fair in his judgement on this and he has written that Bernard by never mentioning Auchinleck's plan of attack but repeatedly mentioning a plan to retreat to the Nile Delta and even abandon Alexandria and Cairo deliberately gave the wrong impression. Say the same thing often enough and most people will believe it. Auchinleck had felt that it was his duty to give the facts to Montgomery about the contingency plan as well as the plans to resume the offensive. Bernard Montgomery harped on to the press and to the Forces about Auchinleck's contingency plan but he refrained from mentioning Auchinleck's (and Gott's) planned offensive thus virtually consigning Auchinleck and Gott to impotence in people's minds. Those in the know, including his own family, were aghast. The public and newly arrived Forces were being hoodwinked into believing that Auchinleck has been on the brink of defeat.

"I have always held that Bernard's condemnation of Auchinleck on this particular point (emphasis on the contingency plan but no mention of plan of attack) **was most unfair and wholly unjustified."**

That appears in Brian Montgomery's book *A Field Marshal in the Family,* on page 269.

Dorman-Smith and other desert commanders strongly challenged Montgomery's insinuations, but Auchinleck had conveniently been sent to India where he maintained a gentlemanly silence on the matter. Everyone connected with the desert had sympathy for Auchinleck and sorrow for Gott but all they could do was fume impotently as the wrong picture emerged and was blindly accepted.

The withdrawal would only have been considered had the situation changed dramatically, and it did not change. Auchinleck's signal to the War Office in London on 31st July 1942 stated, *Situation unchanged*, in other words 'we are still superior by at least 2:1 in men arms and equipment.' This confirmed Auchinleck's signal on 24th July confirming that although there was a contingency plan *it is not likely to arise.*

Auchinleck and Montgomery had previously had policy disagreements but Auchinleck did not have it in him to hold a grudge. Not so Montgomery who went on to criticise Auchinleck's work in India.

Those who were asking in the summer of 1942, 'Why are we waiting' were fed with the excuse that Montgomery was *waiting until he had superior numbers in men, arms and equipment.*

MASSACRE AT ALAMEIN?

A simple study of the state of affairs at that time will show that Montgomery was given 500,000 men in the front line and almost 2000 tanks whereas the Germans had 120,000 men (many of whom were reluctant Italians who would have been much happier as POWs) and 200 tanks, and far inferior air cover to that supplied by the RAF. Sets of figures vary but all sets gave Montgomery superiority.

Despite these figures Montgomery's version was so insidiously orchestrated that it was believed by the troops newly out from England, and it has actually gone down in the annals of history. **It was a lie, and it still is a lie**. It was a cover-up and, sadly, a totally unnecessary cover-up for delay. A simple explanation by Churchill to Auchinleck or Gott and the Alamein advance could have been organised to co-operate with anything Churchill might or might not have managed to arrange with the Americans.

Since the war an acid test is to ask a Desert Warrior serving *before* August 1942 and a Desert Warrior serving *after* August 1942 what he thinks of Bernard Montgomery. The former gives Montgomery the thumbs down, the latter is more likely to give the thumbs up sign.

Colin Roger could not countenance officials and their organisations which were 'going concerns' and had not been created by the Great Colin Roger himself. Thus such long standing and successful activities as sewing classes, football teams, and a strong mens' choir, were gradually sidetracked and replaced by activities which were Colin Roger inspired; like the Boy Bishop, the boys' club and the summer holiday in Ireland.

David Stirling and his friend and avid supporter General Sir John Hackett made an appointment to see Montgomery.

The SAS had added parachute jumping to its bag of tricks because it was admitted that the days of the legendary LRDG patrols would be over once the Battle of Alamein had been won and the Germans removed. The SAS could operate in Europe. That was Stirling's contribution to be offered to Montgomery. Hackett's contribution was the efficient control of Desert Patrol activities from a nerve centre at GHQ Cairo, so that Private Armies did not get in each others' way. The combined efforts of these two men meant that the Germans were confined to the coastal strip and the 8th Army knew exactly where the enemy was. The Afrika Korps could never be sure where the Desert Patrols were operating.

Stirling and Hackett needed a few reinforcements and met Montgomery to finalise arrangements. Auchinleck, Wavell and Gott would never have quibbled because they knew how valuable Stirling's LRDG and SAS contributions were. (Paddy Mayne was in charge of the LRDG in the desert at the time).

Anyone with any sense could see the advantage of harrying the enemy on a nightly basis. Rommel had no equivalent organisation, no 'second army'. He did have a Parachute Brigade under General Ramcke and the Italian Folgore Parachute Division but it would have been suicidal to use them. As early as June Rommel realised that Auchinleck had trapped him and in July Rommel seriously considered pulling his Panzers back to Sollum, to gain freedom of movement, but that would have looked like defeat. It was the British who had freedom of movement. Patrols could destroy aircraft and fuel dumps making Rommel's retreat the more difficult and dangerous. The might of the German Panzers in the desert was something of a myth, their fame being based on the speedy dash across Europe and into Paris. In the desert they were very much ill at ease and rarely attempted to leave the coastline. In his book, 'The Afrika Korps', Ronald Lewin states that 'their invincibility was a lot of moonshine'. Their reputation was sustained by Goebbels' propaganda machine. The same Goebbels, however, was genuinely afraid of the LRDG, threatening death to its members if caught because they were not properly dressed in military uniform and therefore were not protected by the Geneva Convention on the treatment of prisoners of war.

Rommel and Goebbels had tremendous respect for the LRDG and SAS patrols.

Not so Montgomery.

Hard to believe isn't it?

One can only assume that the Montgomery ego could not countenance anything not ordained or created by Montgomery.

How else can his refusal to help Stirling and Hackett be explained?

"You want some of my best men?" he said to Stirling. "I need all my best men here. When I put my plan into operation I shall need every man I can muster."

MASSACRE AT ALAMEIN?

"But, sir, the LRDG and SAS have been operating . . ."

"You think you can use these men better than I can?"

In his book about David Stirling's life Alan Hoe records this episode in these words, *"What, Colonel Stirling, makes you assume that you can handle these men to greater advantage than myself?"*

David Stirling was dumbfounded. He had never intended to cast aspersions on Montgomery's ability to use men. He continued to plead and explain to Montgomery but the general's reply was that if he released any men, "they will miss my offensive which I plan to put into operation very soon."

Montgomery treated Stirling to a sneering look of contempt and told the SAS leader that he was arrogant, concluding with a nasty little jibe about Stirling's failed raid on *Benghazi. This particular raid had been carried out on GHQ's order and against Stirling's advice but Montgomery used it as his final answer to Stirling that, "I cannot tolerate failure!" The pompous little general then held up his hand dismissively and the interview was over.

Stirling was furious and 'Shan' Hackett cooled him down.

On leaving Montgomery's caravan they ran into Freddy de Guingand,

---

Montgomery's cruel jibe referred to a raid on Benghazi planned by GHQ Cairo involving a 'Patrol' augmented to the size of 250 men and 80 to 100 vehicles. This plan was absolutely stupid but David Stirling's better judgement was seduced by the promise of a desert command and that the SAS would be expanded under his control if he played ball. The operation broke every rule of the SAS, it had been planned by 'backroom boys' with no desert experience. There was a furious quarrel between Stirling and the GHQ planners but it became obvious that if David refused he would be replaced and sidelined forever. That evening David Stirling and some other officers were invited to dinner at the British Embassy, and Churchill was there. David, never one to miss an opportunity, discussed the SAS and its role in Europe after the desert campaign was finished, and the Prime Minister was very enthusiastic and supportive. So, although Stirling knew the Benghazi operation was foolhardy he agreed to lead the attack because he knew that the future of the SAS depended on him doing as he was told on this occasion. The Germans 'saw the buffalo-herd' approaching, and David lost 25% of his men and 75% of his vehicles, and achieved nothing . . . except, of course, the permission to go ahead and enlarge the soon-legendary SAS.

MASSACRE AT ALAMEIN?

Montgomery's chief of staff. The two men had known Freddy for many years and were close friends. In no uncertain terms they told Freddy what they thought of his boss. Stirling, by chance, then threw in a remark whose significance he could not have guessed at. "The only hope we have of victory with this man in charge is if the Americans can be persuaded to land in North Africa!" This throwaway line caused Freddy to gasp and Stirling and Hackett were quick witted enough to press Montgomery's chief of staff. Freddy de Guingand could not deny that a second front in North Africa using the Americans was very much on the cards, "but keep your mouths shut!"

In return for keeping their mouths shut David Stirling and Shan Hackett extracted a promise from Freddy that he would keep on pressing the claims of the LRDG and SAS for assistance, and the bargain was struck.

Stirling and Hackett left Montgomery's caravan empty handed except for Freddy's promise of support.

There was also now Churchill's support to fall back on. The Prime Minister called Stirling the 'Scarlet Pimpernel of the Desert', and recommended promotion. David Stirling could plan for the SAS and to Hell with Montgomery!

Continuing the comparison of Bernard with his brother Colin Roger there is the case of the latter causing the removal of 'St John's Own' from the 9th Wallasey boy scouts' shoulder tabs and the even more petty gesture by Bernard in ordering the jerboa sign, mark of the original Desert Rats, to be removed from tanks and vehicles.

The methods used by Montgomery to publicise himself while in the desert were headline catching but as far as the men's welfare was concerned they were empty gestures.

Take early morning PT for example. It is fatal to work oneself up to a state of perspiration in the desert. Fluid is required inside the body, not lost by unnecessary sweating. Normal duties produced more than enough of that. The desert troops were the fittest anywhere in the world. Relaxation had a lot to do with it. Rommel's troops were the ones producing the long lines on Sick Parade. This was almost certainly the result of tension from mental fatigue and disillusionment. Whereas Auchinleck's and Gott's troops could be said to be 'happy', Rommel's were 'sand-happy'. Finally,

105

MASSACRE AT ALAMEIN?

as to fitness in the desert there was not a single Desert Rat who would not have loved the opportunity to say to Montgomery, "All right, sir. We'll each put a pack on our back and march into the blue and see who flakes out first!"

It would never occur to Montgomery to seek the opinion of the troops because he would never admit that they had any right or abilty to make a decision. Desert creatures wake up slowly, letting the sun warm their muscles before they begin to move. Desert Arabs invariably enjoy good health. Swedish Drill belongs to the cold climate of northern Europe.

Giving cigarettes as he stood in his open truck was another empty gesture by Montgomery which made the headlines. What price physical fitness now? Anyway, the troops were given a free issue of 50 'Victory' cigarettes, the most dreadful fags ever made. Even the shoe-shine boys in Cairo would not accept them as currency. But non-smoking Montgomery would not know that, would he?

It was also headline catching when he 'closed the brothels'. What does 'close the brothels' mean in reality? Simply that the Sharia (street) la Berka and Clot Bey area, opposite Shepheards Hotel, in Cairo, and Sister Street in Alexandria were out of bounds to British troops. What Montgomery did not have the wit to understand was that these were officially and medically inspected red light areas and were a mere extension of Saturday night music hall escapism wherein scores of troops on leave, tanked up with Stella beer, visited the area to see the 'exhibitions', in much the same way that charabang loads of old age pensioners view the red light areas of Amsterdam, Berlin, Paris, London . . . and any other great city in the world. The percentage having sex was very small. Montgomery spoilt a good night out for the lads. But, as to Montgomery closing the brothels! . . . as much chance as Canute had of holding back the tide. Lurid posters promising syphillis, gonorrhoea, blindness, insanity and even death from contact with a prostitute put a restraining brake on the red light voyeurs. There was no need for Montgomery's interference.

It is odd how dry-lipped sexless people love to control the sex lives of others.

Montgomery's action was a snub to the Military Medical Authorities, to the Military Police and to the Egyptian Police. Incidentally, Montgomery rubbed in his promotion to Gott's command by physically taking over control 48 hours before he should have done. A snub to Auchinleck, and not a very nice one.

Although Brian Montgomery states that his family had certain characteristics which predominated, not all the nine children were as 'mother-dominated' as Colin Roger and Bernard. It seems that the eldest son, Harold, successfully broke from his mother's apron-strings. In 1931 the family got together at New Park to celebrate Bishop and Lady Montgomery's Golden Wedding. Lady Montgomery found a bottle of gin in Harold's bedroom (he was 47) and there was a terrible fuss. Bishop Montgomery retired to his study. However, Harold was a man in his own right. He loved a gamble, was an excellent horseman, officer, bridge player, was Chief Native Commissioner in Kenya, awarded the CMG, won the respect of the natives and the Arabs, was a kind man, and a very popular man. Not like Colin Roger or Bernard at all. Harold maybe said to his tee-total orison-orientated beldame of a mother, "Ursula and I like a drink before we come down to dinner so, dear mother, will you please put that bottle of gin back where you found it!"

Montgomery never gave any public appreciation of the work Auchinleck and Gott had done in preparing Alamein for victory.

Since January 1942 Auchinleck had been preparing the battlefield of his own choice, Alamein. Secret fortification work had been going on: observation posts, trench and minefield layouts planned, anti-tank ditches in the limestone rock had been dug, piped water had been laid on, a simple railway station at Alamein had been built, there were concrete pillboxes, new anti-tank mines, runways and landing grounds for the RAF, and underground bunkers. (This was the activity which the Alamein Canal enthusiasts hoped to use if Alamein was not required as a battlefield). In May Rommel had 'won a victory' at Gazala and this had lifted his morale but when he arrived at Alamein he was clever enough to see that he had been led into a carefully prepared ambush and his brief moments of hope quickly evaporated. Auchinleck was not going to fight at Gazala. He was going to fight where he had planned, at Alamein.

The first Battle of Alamein took place during the blazing heat of the

MASSACRE AT ALAMEIN?

desert during July. Rommel was desperate, Auchinleck was resolute. The desert heat won. The fighting stopped and Rommel returned west of the Alamein Line and on July 27th Auchinleck's chief of staff sent to the War Office in London a typically modest and laconic appreciation of the situation at Alamein: *The Axis is unlikely to secure a decisive majority over Eighth Army... they are hardly strong enough to attempt the conquest of the Delta.*

The students in Cairo yelled for a German victory, but the hotels of Mena, Cairo and Alexandria were unimpressed and continued 'business as usual'.

Rommel had already written to his wife that 'there are no more medals to be won in the desert'. Now he wrote to his German commanders that 'there were no more laurels to be won in the desert'. And no more reinforcements, except a few and many of those were ex-seamen from a Merchant Navy without ships.

Gott took over from Auchinleck, everything nicely in place.

Then, a German bullet with Gott's name on it changed everything.

'But for this we would never have heard of Montgomery!' (Oberleutnant Heinz Schmidt, a desert commander under Rommel.)

MONTGOMERY

CHAPTER ELEVEN

Montgomery's Folly at Alamein.
How the Battle Should Have Been Fought.

Several decades after World War Two had ended Bernard Montgomery was being interviewed at his home at Islington Mill in Alton, Hampshire, and in answer to a question concerning General Auchinleck the Viscount Montgomery of Alamein showed no mellowing through age when he replied dismissively in his crisp but affected voice, "Too political! Too much Indian Army!"

The two points in that terse reply are most revealing.

Take the second point, the one about the Indian Army.

This is pure jealousy.

Bernard Montgomery did not get into the Indian Army because he was not marked high enough at his training (Sandhurst & Royal Military College).

His brother Brian wrote that it had always been assumed that Bernard would follow the family tradition and join the Indian Army (if not the Church). Only the best cadet officers at Sandhurst were enrolled and this elite corps of young men did not include Bernard. Sir Robert Montgomery, GCSI, KCB, 1809–1887, his grandfather, had become famous in the Indian Army and Bernard's failure to follow the line was a personal and family disappointment.

The first point of his reply, about Auchinleck being 'too political', is a more subtle issue and a brief explanation of the military-cum-political situation in Egypt in 1942 will serve to illustrate Montgomery's ignorance of the necessary partnership and co-operation of the British Embassy (political) and GHQ, Cairo (military). As a consequence he failed to appreciate the intricacies of Auchinleck's 'contingency plan', which he continuously rubbished by doggedly declaring to troops, press, fellow officers, and War Office in London, that "there will be no more withdrawals!" In other words, there will be no use made of Auchinleck's contingency plan.

Here are some reasons why Auchinleck's contingency plan was essential, and why the plan had to be both military and political.

There was a real danger lurking in Egypt which the British had to guard against. The individual friendships between British and Egyptian people (including King Farouk and several British officers) in no way lessened the hatred the Egyptian nation had for the colonial-style occupation by the British armed forces. A national revolt was always there, just under the surface, waiting for the right spark to set it alight.

When Auchinleck in January 1942 began the military preparation for the Alamein Ambush he knew that there was also an essential and urgent political preparation to be engineered to defuse an Egyptian rebellion.

In January 1942 it was realised that the Egyptian Government was becoming (not surprisingly) very 'Bolshie'.

The King, diplomatically approached, refused to appoint a more British-minded Prime Minister and so, in February 1942, there was the infamous *coup de grace* when Sir Miles Lampson and his tanks entered the gates of King Farouk's Abdin Palace and forced him to appoint the more moderate Nahas Pasha as Prime Minister.

The whole of Egypt simmered in repressed anger at this double humiliation of King and Parliament.

One of the most dangerous anti-British groups was in the Egyptian Army, the Free Officers Organization. It had leaders such as Gamal Nasser and Anwar el-Sadat. These angry and imaginative young officers had to be contained, and the British took action to see that this was done.

In November 1941 Nasser's battalion was near Mersa Matruh, but Nasser himself was not there. He was posted to the far reaches of Upper Egypt and finally given a posting in the Sudan where he remained until December 1942, i.e., after Alamein.

Sadat was more brutally treated, spending 1941 under intense interrogation and confinement and then imprisoned in the Aliens' Prison. (While Sadat was in prison Nasser took over command of the clandestine Free Officers Organization.) Egypt's Field Marshal Ahmed Ismail Ali, although devoted to his military career, supported the Free Officers and attended their meetings.

The British, through the work of Russell Pasha, had a great deal of control over the Egyptian police.

Thus, with King, Government, Army and Police under tight control only the students were left to cry anti-British slogans in the streets of Cairo and Alexandria.

In their young voices was heard the true voice of a suppressed Egypt: "Advance Rommel!" A German victory would drive the British out of their country. Under these conditions the advance of Rommel was treated by the Egyptians as a Godsend.

Therein lay the political danger.

If Egypt and Rommel could forge a partnership then it would tip the balance Rommel's way because the Egyptian Army, Government, King, and population would rise in unison plus, of course, the Italians in the desert who would take renewed interest in the war. Mussolini saw the possibility and actually renewed his vision of an Italian Empire and, showman to the last, he decided for a second time that he would ride into Cairo on a white horse just as they used to do in the heady days of the Roman Empire. If Rommel could get to Alexandria the odds would definitely then be on the German side and the British would lose the advantage they had at Alamein.

Sadat saw danger for Egypt, however, that if a deal with Rommel was not formally acknowledged Egypt might lose one master and gain another. He drew up a treaty to present to Rommel. It pointed out that the Egyptians were also fighting the British and that the entire Egyptian Army and Air Force would be put at Rommel's disposal. Sadat also promised air-photos of all the British positions and in addition the Egyptian Army would not let one British soldier leave Cairo.

What did Sadat want in return? Independence for Egypt. Hitler had already promised Farouk that he would be leader of the Arab countries.

MASSACRE AT ALAMEIN?

Therein lay the threat of an anti-British Arab uprising also involving Palestine, a country which knew it would get a better Arab-Jew deal from the Germans than from the British. Sadat was twenty-two at the time and he and Nasser and the other leaders of the Free Officers had been friends and conspirators for three years. They were sharpening their political skills.

Sadat's treaty, endorsed by his Free Officers colleagues, included Abdel Munim Abdul-Rauf, Abdel Latif al-Baghdadi, Hassan Ibrahim, Khaled Mohieddin, Ahmed Saudi Hussein (pilot), and Hassan Izzat.

The treaty and the air-photos were placed in a bag and Ahmed Saudi Hussein was ordered to fly to Alamein where Rommel had been alerted. Ahmed flew in a British Gladiator but the signal was misunderstood and the plane was shot down by the Germans and Hussein was killed.

However, this was not the only attempt to contact Rommel officially. Two German spies, using desert camel routes, got into Cairo and approached Sadat. One of these was Eppler who had a German mother and an Egyptian High Court judge for father. The second German was called 'Sandy'. He could not speak a word of Arabic and his English was suspect. The British had been alerted by their own desert Intelligence contacts to the presence of these two Germans but what particularly gave them away was a reckless gambling spree in night clubs and cabarets where large sums of money were spent. The Germans lived on a houseboat rented to them by the night club singer Hikmat Fahmi. At the time Sadat was out of prison and living in the Kubri al-Qubbah district of Cairo.

The two spies offered Captain Sadat the opportunity to contact Rommel at Alamein. On the houseboat was a slightly damaged wireless transmitter which Sadat took to his home for repair.

Eppler and Sandy were arrested and Sadat's home visited.

Men are not allowed by religious tradition to enter a room occupied by female members of a family. In that room was the wireless transmitter. Nothing was found at Sadat's home but his movements were closely watched. Eppler incriminated Sadat because the British said they would spare Eppler's life if he confessed everything. He betrayed Sadat who was stripped of his rank and placed in the Aliens' Jail. In the solitude which a prison cell can offer Anwar el-Sadat continued his plotting for the defeat of the British and the revolution within Egypt, to create an Egypt free of all foreign domination.

This revolution actually took place in 1952 but, with Rommel's help, could it take place in 1942? With the help of the charismatic Rommel the 1952 revolution might have taken place in 1942, Alamein would have been lost and the British expelled.

Auchinleck's 'contingency plan', which Montgomery so scorned, was designed both militarily and politically to make sure that no such Egyptian or Arab revolution took place in 1942. That meant that Rommel must not by-pass the Alamein Line and reach Alexandria. If he did, however, Auchinleck still had plans to thwart the Germans by using forces stationed in the Nile Delta. Rommel had tried and failed to break through in the first Battle of Alamein in July.

Now, with a new British General in charge, it was certain that Rommel would have one more go. His 1942 arrival in Alexandria would be even more triumphant and significant than his 1940 arrival in Paris. It could spark off an Egyptian revolution and the British would be outnumbered.

One of Auchinleck's trump cards in the contingency plan would be the LRDG and SAS patrols who would cut off the supply route for supplies and support between Rommel's main army and his advance group who had managed to reach Alexandria. Not only that but the British troops in the Delta had been alerted to such a danger so, even if the imaginative Rommel did get a few armoured trucks to enter Alexandria, the British would prevent any military liaison between Rommel and Egypt. The Egyptian's teeth had been drawn politically; they had a lame duck King, an impotent Parliament, an army whose leading young officers were under arrest, and a police force undecided which way to turn. (Their officers, individually, had powerful jobs which they were reluctant to put carelessly in jeopardy. They wanted to keep their rank and jobs no matter who dominated Egypt. Their task would be to keep public order and restrain as much as possible such things as looting, arson and murder in the mayhem of a revolution).

Auchinleck was political, as Montgomery said. The sad thing was that Montgomery did not know what 'political' meant. He never was a bright student either at school or at military college and his thoughtless comment that Auchinleck was 'too political' confirms his ignorance of what was really going on in Egypt and the Middle East in general. Montgomery's attitude was still, "Have we killed enough Arabs to keep the area quiet?"

As a matter of fact one wonders if even the great man himself, Churchill, understood the complexities of the Middle East because he said (in his book, The Second World War) ". . . that everyone in uniform (in the Middle East) must fight exactly as they would if Kent or Sussex were invaded."

The word *exactly* makes this absolute nonsense. Fighting in Kent and Sussex is fighting on one's own territory. Fighting in the desert was fighting on someone else's territory. Kent and Sussex have civilians, hospitals, houses, schools, factories, roads, hills, rivers, and the occasional forest to circumnavigate; the desert is as open as a football pitch. In England one is lucky to see even two miles ahead, in the clear air of the desert one's eyes soon focus on distances of twenty or thirty miles. There is an enormous, and unique, difference between fighting in England (or Europe) and in the desert and the method of fighting is reflected in this difference.

On the other hand, Churchill fully appreciated the necessity and the thoroughness of Auchinleck's contingency plan and ordered Montgomery to ask about this on arrival in Egypt. Montgomery's subsequent arrogant dismissal of the plan was because he was not bright enough to understand that in the Middle East one *had* to be political as well as military minded.

Montgomery knew he had more men than Rommel, so, what's the problem?

If only war on foreign soil were as simple as that!

There was little doubt in anyone's mind that Rommel would make a second attempt to break through Auchinleck's Alamein Line, now protected by this new man, Montgomery.

The Germans opened the second Battle of Alamein on 31st August, 1942.

Rommel made the almost mandatory feint in the north of the Line by a mock bombardment, to tie up as many British troops there as possible. Only a fool or madman would attempt the World War One tactic of head-on collision by attacking the northern end of the Alamein Line and

MASSACRE AT ALAMEIN?

gaining, say, one hundred yards for the loss of 10,000 lives. The Alamein area was safely guarded by the wonderful 9th Australian Division and the experienced 1st South African Division.

Rommel's real attack was, of course, in the south and the 21st and 15th Panzer Divisions tried to crash their way through the Himeimat central section and then attempt to win the Alam el Halfa Ridge, held by the 44th Home Counties Division, recently arrived in the desert, plus the 10th Armoured Division.

The battle would be for control of Alam el Halfa, ten miles east of Alamein.

Under the cover of this battle the area even further to the south provided a possible route for a small German patrol to sneak past the main area of fighting and it would only be an hour's drive into Alexandria. The arrival of such a patrol, especially if Rommel was with it, could spark off an Egyptian uprising and if the Egyptians were quickly organised and drove towards Alamein from Alexandria, and north west from Cairo, then it would be the British who would be ambushed at Alamein and not the Germans. A full Arab uprising would then be a terrifying prospect for the British.

Rommel's most southerly Panzers did indeed attempt an advance some 30 miles inland and well south of the main battle but this danger area was covered by the late General Gott's men of the 7th Armoured Division and they held firm. Hence, as a deserved tribute to the luckless Strafer Gott the headline **GOTT'S GHOST ROUTS ROMMEL** is advocated in this book as a memorial to a great desert fighter.

To the north, at Alam el Halfa, Montgomery's new men were fighting bravely and the Germans were held, then driven back, and it was all over for the Germans by September 7th.

Rommel's diaries, letters to his wife, and reports to Berlin confirm that he knew Alamein was a battle he could not now possibly win. As far back as July 1st he had written to his wife, "Resistance is too great and our strength is exhausted", and at about the same time Major-General von Mellenthin wrote, "We have failed!", and Rommel and his senior officers knew this to be true and everything they did from then on reflected this belief.

115

MASSACRE AT ALAMEIN?

Rommel could never understand why Montgomery did not follow up his Alam el Halfa success, and from a British point of view had Rommel been driven westwards from Alamein mass surrenders would have occurred because history discloses that Rommel did not have enough petrol for full retreat of his army. Had Montgomery acted as any normal person and chased Rommel there would have been no need for the third Battle of Alamein at the end of October. The German retreat in September need not necessarily have damaged any secret negotiations Churchill was having with the Americans. Thousands of prisoners would have been taken and ultimately many lives saved. Axis casualties were 3000 to the 8th Army's 2000 and losses in aircraft and armoured vehicles were about even in the second Battle of Alamein. One is left to wonder if this comparatively gentle (in loss of life) victory is what Churchill wanted? Did he want something more bloodthirsty? Was it Churchill who told Montgomery to hold his horses? Did he want to hear Montgomery say the equivalent of, "have I killed enough troops to keep Stalin quiet?" Churchill was desperate for American and Russian co-operation. Roosevelt wanted time and Stalin wanted blood.

Under Montgomery the troops felt rather bewildered. Relations between men who had fought under Wavell and Auchinleck versus those newly arrived was understandably alien and would pass with time, but there were new tensions.

The 'elite club' mentality of the Desert Rats solidarity which did so much for morale gradually gave way to mistrust; infantry and armour became notoriously antagonistic towards each other, and feelings between the various arms of the service became less harmonious. The newspapers gave a wrong impression by asserting that Montgomery was re-training these men to become 'one army'. In truth the men felt that it had been 'their war' under Wavell and Auchinleck and Gott but under Montgomery it was becoming 'his war', and this was hurtful.

Montgomery courted the favour of the press and particularly that of Geoffrey Keating's Army and Photographic Unit who filmed the general in a variety of eye-catching gear until it was decided that the black beret with *two* badges, a scruffy sweater and baggy trousers created the correct rakish touch for desert warfare. In short, he was copying the Desert Rats with their inabstinent appearance, careless loose-limbed way of moving, handsomely burnt by the sun, brimming with good health and self-confidence that made them sing as they went along, proud to be the 'Desert Rats'.

His schoolboy nickname, 'Monkey Montgomery', would never do so he saw to it that the press continually referred to him by the more flattering *nom de guerre,* Monty.

He had a favourite trick and that was to invite a group of men to break ranks and sit on the ground at his feet while he told them that they had had a bad time (before 'I' was in charge) and that those days were gone (now 'I' am in charge) and now, "We'll fight like a pwoper army and we'll knock Wommel for six, wight out of Afwica!"

Can you imagine Auchinleck 'knocking' Wavell like that in front of his men, or Gott knocking Auchinleck at the second changeover of leadership?

Auchinleck had been sacked because he insisted on waiting until September 9th before attacking the Germans at Alamein. What a wonderful choice of date it had become now because by September 9th the Germans were in complete disarray having lost their second battle against the British at Alamein. This time they really were *mafeesh benzine!,* without the means of further transport until, and if, supplies arrived.

Why was Montgomery refusing to take this golden opportunity to finish the Battle of Alamein once and for all? The delay bewildered Rommel, and angered the sun-tanned and experienced Desert Rats. The public at large was being fed with reports that Montgomery was 'waiting until he had superior forces' and that he was 'building up the morale of the 8th Army'. **This is very plausible when seen in print, so plausible that these lies have gone down in military history** as evidence that Montgomery was 'an excellent leader' and one who 'cared for the welfare of his men', one who would make sure he had 'superior arms and numbers' before he struck.

An Egyptian member of the Nationalistic Wafd Party optimistically expecting to see lorry loads of defeated, dejected and dismayed British troops entering and leaving Cairo was disillusioned by what he actually saw and reported so to the Egyptian press. "The dust covered soldiers did not look panic-stricken. There was raucous singing. When a lorry stopped the soldiers jumped out, got a fire going and made themselves tea while others noisily kicked a football around."

Montgomery's behaviour far from stiffening morale of the 8th Army caused some alarm by his barn-storming utterances. A hitherto unknown soldier later named by the writer James Lucas as R.P. Hill of the RASC was one of many who were worried by the World War One tone of Montgomery's Battle Order. Phrases such as, 'We will hit them for six!' did not have the elevating effect Montgomery hoped for. Sir Brian Horrocks, writing for the 'News of the World' in 1967, confessed that "it would be wrong to say that the morale of the 8th Army at that time was bad." Feelings would have been mutually improved if Montgomery had adopted a more friendly and appreciative approach.

Experts were alarmed when it was known that the 'Montgomery attack' would not use a flanking 'sweep'. 'What,' many wondered, 'about Rommel's "Devil's Garden" and the deadly 88mm guns at the northern end?'

The Germans made good use of the time Montgomery was allowing them. An enormous minefield which they named 'The Devil's Garden' was constructed west of Alamein. Its size varied from two to five miles in width and they had actually completed the whole length to the Qattara Depression before Montgomery struck on October 23rd. This was all against what Auchinleck had planned. He would never have allowed the Germans to dig in and thus ruin the effect of the Alamein Ambush. It was getting more and more to look like World War One trench warfare; slow, ponderous, and terribly lethal. In the desert speed of movement was essential. There were no hiding places for the slow. There was little else for the Germans to do except dig in because Rommel had told his men that it was inevitable but they had to stand and prepare for the worst. This they did with mines and booby traps.

'At least,' Rommel's men knew, 'that if anyone is stupid enough to attack us at the north end of the line they'll get more than they bargained for.' It would also slow up Montgomery's advance because a detour would be necessay for the bulk of his vast army. **The longer Montgomery waited the more defensive work the Germans would be able to complete.**

MASSACRE AT ALAMEIN?

Many were annoyed by Montgomery's ability to isolate himself. He would shut himself up in his caravan at Burg al Arab from '6 p.m. until 6 a.m.'

Montgomery did not attract the affection which had been given to Wavell and Auchinleck, despite what the papers said. Montgomery became known to his men by reputation (press and news-film coverage) rather than by sight. Newcomers to the desert, however, held Montgomery in reverence. A situation not unlike his brother Colin Roger's arrival at his church in Wallasey; devisive, the established against the new.

Personal visits to his men invariably had press and film coverage. There *was* friction between men in the 8th Army but it developed after Montgomery arrived and was, therefore, of his own making. There was deep resentment that this new commander was showing no appreciation for the work his predecessors had done. He was being handed victory at Alamein on a plate and he was not even saying 'Thank you' to those who had prepared the victory-winning scenario.

It was on September 9th 1942 that Rommel sent yet another message to Berlin that unless there was a dramatic change in his favour there was 'no chance of victory, and the Panzerarmee will suffer the fate of the Halfaya garrison' (a reference to the time Halfaya was isolated and easily captured by the British). The Germans knew that the strangely hesitant Montgomery would attack sooner or later and Rommel christened the coming encounter 'The Battle Without Hope' (from, of course, the German point of view).

Much of Rommel's food supplies were not from Germany but were those captured from the British at Tobruk, Matruh, and various dumping grounds, but this food was now exhausted. Little was coming from Germany and Italy and the Luftwaffe pilots were required elsewhere. The RAF Desert Air Force under Air Marshal Tedder had a monopoly, although the German pilots still in the desert were too dangerous to ignore. In the Med. the tally of Axis sinkings rose: six ships in June, seven in July, and twelve in August. For the British new and stronger American Sherman tanks plus more British Crusader tanks had arrived and also new anti-tank guns and 105 Howitzers. Because the British were near base, Alexandria, they could be rotated to offset the hygiene problems of staying in the same

MASSACRE AT ALAMEIN?

place for too long, and they had a very effective AL63 anti-lice powder.

For the Axis it was continually reported that the sickness ratio for such complaints as jaundice, desert sores, gastro-enteritis and exhaustion were increasing and sick parades were becoming longer by the day. The British Field Hygiene Section reported on the verminous condition of captured Axis soldiers.

Rommel was having fainting fits, and during the Alam el Halfa battle Ronald Lewin reports that Rommel was so ill he could hardly get in or out of a tank. On September 23rd, still surprised that Montgomery had not struck he went on sick leave to Germany, leaving Generals von Thoma and Stumme (from Russia) in charge. General Stumme was a sick man with a heart complaint and he was now the one up against Montgomery. Von Thoma was also war-weary from service in Russia. An authoritive estimate at the time gave Montgomery 195,000 men against Stumme's 104,000 (half of whom were half-hearted Italians). So much for the press coverage that Montgomery was waiting for superiority in numbers.

Rommel did return to the desert in late September but Goebbels had been thinking. Things had not been going well for Germany in Europe and Russia and there were signs of unrest among the German population. Had Montgomery struck on Auchinleck's date of September 9th the resultant victory would have had a catostrophic effect on German morale but Rommel had been spared a conclusive defeat so far. The German population needed a pep talk so Goebbels arranged for Rommel to be called back to Germany to give a morale-boosting talk, a-la-Churchill if possible. On October 3rd Rommel spoke to the German people, "Our troops in the desert are magnificent. Our Allies, Italy, are magnificent!" and so on. (This was partly true because General Stumme was deliberately praising the Italians, reminding them of the glories of the Roman Empire, and trying to give them back their self-respect and will to fight.)

Goebbels was nothing if not cunning so he persuaded Rommel and Hitler that the German national hero, Erwin Rommel, should remain in Germany on sick leave for the whole of October. Montgomery could not dither forever so when the British did strike at Alamein Rommel would not be there to be beaten and his reputation as Germany's hero would not be unduly damaged. His fame might be used to greater effect in Russia, and Rommel was the kind of flamboyant soldier who thrived on the big stage and he might therefore relish the task of reviving Germany's hopes of beating Stalin by serving on the Russian front. Postwar papers confirm that Hitler did have plans to use Rommel against Russia, in the Ukraine.

The fact remains that while Montgomery prepared to beat the enigmatic 'Rommel' the German field marshal was in Germany throughout October and he was still there when the third Battle of Alamein began on the night of October 23rd 1942.

During the day the formations had been lining up in their assigned Battle Order and Montgomery moved to his tactical headquarters close behind 10 and 30 Corps controlled by General Lumsden and Lt.-General Sir Oliver Leese respectively. At 21.40 hours a terrific artillery barrage opened with an intensity not seen since World War One. Over 900 guns belched out their lethal shells and this Hell-raising firework display continued for five and a half hours.

The attacking infantry of 30 Corps (better referred to as XXX Corps) was ordered to creep forward through the minefields.

James Lucas ('War in the Desert') pointed out that this mighty bombardment with infantry advancing slowly on foot brought back to the older men in the desert, 'memories and experiences of barrages fired during the Battles of the Somme and of Passchendaele'.

There is no doubt that Montgomery in the lonely nights in his caravan had 'done his homework' and there was little about German positions he did not know. His words before the battle were nothing more than a truism, "Battles are won before they are fought, and this battle is already won!"

Auchinleck and Gott could have said exactly the same thing because of the careful planning *they* had done.

But, what a difference in the two plans. We shall never know for certain what the cost of the Auchinleck/Gott plan would have been in lives. We only know that Auchinleck and Gott would have opted for speed and a fast flanking movement. All we can do is present the two plans and pose the question: Was Montgomery's plan a needless massacre?

We begin by taking the plan of attack Montgomery had for XXX Corps. The commander, Oliver Leese, was newly out from England and was not, therefore, in an experienced desert position to argue with Montgomery. The Order of Battle (a diagram copy of which I have before me as I write) is all four-square and neat and tidy and well-researched. The lines of the diagram are straight and the various brigades are lined up smartly in order, row behind row.

In front, lined up side by side in the diagram, are 51st Division, 2nd New Zealand Division, and 4th Indian Division. Behind this front row are more lines of men producing a second row of: 152nd Brigade, 9th Armoured Brigade, and 5th Brigade. On the third row are the 153rd Brigade, 5th New Zealand Brigade, and 7th Brigade, and on the fourth row are the 154th Brigade, 6th New Zealand Brigade, and the 161st Brigade.

Behind this assembly of brigades Montgomery placed the 9th Australian Division and 1st South African Division, with three rows of brigades behind this front row. On the second row are the 20th Brigade and 1st Brigade, third row has the 24th Brigade and 2nd Brigade, and finally on the fourth row are the 26th and 3rd Brigades.

The 'Held in Reserve' list includes: 23rd Armoured Brigade Group, 4/6th South African Armoured Car Regiment, 7th, 64th, and 69th Field Regiments, 8th, 40th, 46th and 50th Royal Tank Regiment, 121st Field Regiment, Royal Artillery, 168th Light Anti-Aircraft Battery, 195th Army Field Company, Royal Engineers.

A similar meticulously prepared Order of Battle was prepared for XIII Corps, whose former O.C. was Gott himself. This was now led by another man freshly out from England and therefore unacquainted with the desert, Brian Horrocks, and this is a point worth bearing in mind while considering the feasibility of Montgomery's Plan. XIII Corps has the Home Counties 44th Division, the experienced 7th Armoured Division (another of Gott's successful 'desert groups', with General Harding now in command), and the 50th Division on the front row, with three rows of brigades behind them. A similar pattern to that of XXX Corps.

There is also a plan for X Corps, under General Lumsden who was anything but happy about the scheme. His leaders were the 1st Armoured Division and the 10th Armoured Division (led by General Gatehouse who also had doubts about the Montgomery strategy), supported by the 2nd Armoured Brigade, 7th Motor Brigade, and the 8th Armoured Brigade with the 24th Armoured Brigade and the 133rd Lorried Infantry Brigade were in the rear.

The amount of 'homework' gone into this Montgomery Plan was, at first sight, most impressive for the new arrivals, for the press and film crews, and for reports back to the War Office. For those experienced in desert warfare, however, this was 'Fields of Flanders' stuff; slow, murderous creeping over the killing Sands of Alamein.

The men of the desert would have followed the lead of Wavell, Auchinleck, Gott and Rommel who would have opted, on the second day, to sweep under and upwards round the enemy's rear. Gott would have moved some of his men *behind the* Axis lines, thus surrounding them and completing the ambush carefully planned during the whole of 1942. After the opening salvo they would not have trudged step by dying step into their own ambush and on to Rommel's reinforced minefields where tanks were sitting ducks for the gunners.

Speed. The desert calls out for speed when the battle opens. Speed and imagination. Sweep up behind with a three-pronged attack, cut off supplies and reserves, but, Montgomery had rudely eschewed Stirling's help with LRDG and SAS patrols. (Actually, they ignored Montgomery and carried on with the raids and demolition work as of yore. To illustrate one difference of opinion between Montgomery and his immediate superior, General Alexander, rather than belittle Stirling General Alexander on asking how many men Stirling had and being told four hundred he replied to David Stirling, "You should really have four thousand!" Stirling explained that LRDG patrols operated better in small numbers.)

With the men Montgomery had at his disposal and faced by an Axis army of only half that number the simple mathematical thinking could be: "If I place 100 men exchanging fire with 50 men, when 50 men on each side have killed each other the opposite side will have no men left but I shall have 50!"

Such a plan was a reckless misuse of human life. Montgomery could, of course, point to Leningrad. When the figures were released it showed that 1,000,000 died in the merciless bombardment. Was this the sort of thing he and Churchill wanted? After all, Churchill was a bulldog not a dove and all he wanted from Montgomery was the expected 'Victory'.

There were not only men in the forces who doubted Montgomery's tactics but also some of the press who had seen Wavell and Auchinleck and Rommel in action and doubted if Montgomery was acting in the best way possible. Christopher Buckley, writing in the Daily Telegraph, was worried about the need for such a prolonged barrage, stating that it was 'like one of the vast conflicts of 1914–18'.

Montgomery had at the extreme north of the Alamein Line the tremendously brave and experienced fighters, the 9th Australians, comrades of the famous Desert Rats who held on to Tobruk. In the extreme south next to the Qattara Depression were the Free French, and if we review the line-up going from the north down to the south, i.e. a distance of some 30 miles, we see immediately south of the Australians the 51st Division, then the 2nd New Zealand Division, and then the 1st South African Division.

They were faced by the 15th Panzers, two Italian Light Divisions and the Trento Division.

In the front line of the central section of the Alamein Line were the 4th Indian Division (augmented by Greek soldiers immediately south) and 50th Division, faced by the 21st Panzers and three Italian Divisions, and in the south immediately above the Free French were the 44th Division and the 7th Armoured Division faced by the Folgore Parachute Division and the Pavia Division.

There were also Axis minefields there which had been placed in the September 7th to October 23rd period which Montgomery had presented gratis to the Axis forces by his prolonged delay. It becomes ever more clear how wise Auchinleck was in his choice of September 9th to launch the Big Push! Rommel would have had no time to lay his murderous minefields.

The 1st Armoured Division had orders to clear the minefields at the Miteiriya Ridge, entering enemy ground between where the 1st South African Division and the 4th Indian Division were stationed. Apart from the minefields they soon came up against the Tranto, Littorio and Bologna Divisions and progress was slower than Montgomery had anticipated. The lanes cleared in the minefields were so narrow the tanks had to remain in line, with absolutely no room for manoeuvre. They were at the mercy of the Italian gunners and the deadly German 88mm guns.

In the south XIII Corps was soon in difficulties and unable to achieve its objective, i.e., to pass a light armoured force through the Alam Nayil Ridge. Their commander, Lt.-General Horrocks, later described it as a **"slogging match on the lines of some battle fought during the 1914–18 war"**.

The 10th Armoured Division, too, was having difficulty. Apart from the solid wall of minefields Rommel had had time to build he had also scattered mines all over the place and these were causing chaos and, worse, congestion. In the middle of a minefield with hundreds of guns blazing away a traffic jam was the last thing the Empire Forces wanted. Writing a letter home two weeks after the final battle had ended (in November) one soldier wrote, 'as the tanks burnt all I could think was, "Christ help those poor sods inside".' RSM Lindley wrote, 'we suffered heavy casualties,' and a Frank Compton wrote, 'the most miserable moment of my life was seeing our tanks being decimated by the German 88s.'

The initial advance had to be completed before dawn broke because of the open nature of the desert but with the congestion it was obvious that the Allies were going to be trapped in an ambush of their own making. It had been considered that Alamein was a battle even the inexperienced Montgomery could not lose but if dawn was going to display his advance forces trapped in a massive minefield then the German and Italian gunners would have a field day and the numerical balance Montgomery held would be seriously altered in the Axis' favour. Because of the dark, errors were made. For example, men were unable to locate their positions accurately and as a result the assault lanes of the Queens' (who had to be relieved by units of the Kent Brigade) and the Sappers moved in different directions creating an area between the two tracks for the enemy snipers to cause heavy losses to Montgomery's forward troops. Rommel had taught his men to fire smoke at the exits to minefields and this ploy silhouetted the emerging tanks and made them easy targets for the German and Italian gunners. 'C' Squadron of the County of London Yeomanry was wiped out in minutes. Flames and smoke marked the burning of the tanks of the 22nd Armoured Brigade. Much of the British shell fire bounced off the German tanks. Not so in the case of the British vehicles. The terrible 88mm bullets

MASSACRE AT ALAMEIN?

of the Germans travelled at such speed that they hit their target almost before the tracer-like flash had been seen. Montgomery had such reserves of 'units' (a unit being a man's life) that he knew even the most terrific losses in the night could be sustained.

As tank after tank was knocked out and the desert was filled with men screaming and trying to get clear of burning vehicles. The infantry cursed the immobilised tanks for drawing the enemy fire, but how can even a mobile tank conceal itself? How can a tank crew escape from a burning vehicle?

"Mother! Christ! I'm on fire!"

"Help! Somebody help me! I'm burning!"

"I'm trapped! For Christ's sake, somebody shoot me! We're all burning!"

General Lumsden and other commanders could see that Montgomery's plan to be in an attacking position by morning was not going to work, not unless almost every man was wiped out and the reinforcements advanced over their dead bodies. The night was not going to plan. Men were dying by the hundred and no real advance was being won. Should the men regroup? Should they continue to advance into almost certain death? It was night. The desert moon at night can be strong enough for one to read a letter, certainly bright enough for one to see a hundred yards ahead. It was the smoke of fire and the scream of shells which disorientated the lost souls that terrible night. On a normal night one can stand in the nocturnal desert and look up into eternity; countless billions of stars, galaxies such as Andromeda and The Milky Way are clearly visible. They seem near enough to touch. From a tiny segment of the desert one can look and see forever and ever into limitless space. It is awe-inspiring, mind-broadening, utterly magnificent.

The night of October 23/24th 1942 was not one for such dreaming. As the inevitable dawn approached the men fought to retain a semblance of sanity. Subsequently, letters home grasping for words to describe the intensity of the fear, wrote of the sound of bagpipes wailing over the desert battlefield. 152/153/154 Brigades included famous Scottish regiments: The Black Watch, The Highland Division, The Gordons, The Argyll and Sutherland, et al. Some letters home claimed that the tunes of 'Road to the

MASSACRE AT ALAMEIN?

Isles' could be distinguished, and 'Highland Laddie', and one letter wrote of the sound of a lone piper playing a dawn lament for the dead of Alamein. Another wrote, 'My hands did not stop shaking for eight weeks!'

The seasoned desert commanders, knowing that objectives had not been achieved in the murderous chaos of the night wondered in vain if Montgomery had an alternative plan, a contingency plan. Seemingly not. In the morning Montgomery seemed strangely unmoved, self-satisfied. He saw no need for any change to His Plan.

He reckoned he did not need one with the vast reserves of 'units' at his disposal. He did not have a War Council of experienced desert commanders. There were famous leaders at the front who knew 'every inch of the desert' but, although Montgomery had never seen the other side of Alamein, he did not seek their advice. It was his plan and he dictator-like would make all the decisions.

By morning many lives had been lost, the Miteiriya Ridge had not been occupied (it took a further two days), Montgomery was still where he had been the day before, the German leader Erwin Romell was in Germany, General Stumme the Number Two had a heart attack during the bombardment and died, the Chief of Staff Bayerlein was on leave, in fact on the morning of October 24th the Germans in the desert were completely leaderless and it is to the credit of 15th Panzer Division in the north and the 21st coming up from the south that they stood up so valiently to Montgomery's massive army of tanks and held the Ridge the Allies so desperately wanted to gain control of.

There is much to be said for not altering a formation once it has been set up and, to give Montgomery his due, it was correct not to higgledy-piggledy allow groups of men to break ranks no matter how serious the position became. This rigidity, however, can become flexible in desert warfare because the battlefield is open ground. The position on the morning of October 24th screamed out for the southern formations (possibly the 7th Armoured Division, Free French Brigade or the 44th Division), to sweep west and then north, through the defence formations of the Italian Pavia, Folgore and Ariete Divisions and get *behind* the enemy lines as near to the coast as possible.

Behind the Miteiriya Ridge was another called Kidney Ridge and it is behind that area that an imaginative desert commander would have aimed on October 24th. Luck would have favoured the brave because the 21st Panzers were called away to help in the defence against Montgomery's tank and infantry attack on the night of October 23rd. (The 7th Armoured Division did occupy this area eventually but by then it was November 4th and the direction had been head-on over dead bodies and not in a typical desert flanking movement early on, say, on October 24th or 25th) . If el Daba on the coast could be reached then the Alamein Ambush would have been complete, as per the planning and thinking of Auchinleck and Gott and, indeed, of Rommel.

Rommel's men had expected an unbeatable six-pronged attack; a three-pronged land attack, an air attack, a naval bombardment, and the sixth that of the unpredictable LRDG and SAS patrols, the desert commanders' Second Army. Speed and imagination combined.

Imagination was not Montgomery's strong suit. How can a man be so unimaginative as to say that, "all a woman needs is a serviceable dress and a waterproof hat"? How can a man be so unimaginative as not to co-operative with the famous LRDG and SAS Patrols? "Do you, Stirling, think you can use my best men better than I can?" was Montgomery's attitude.

On the day Auchinleck opened the 1941/42 battle he had a special patrol which attempted to capture Rommel. Imaginative. Daring. Dangerous but romantic in the true tradition of desert fighting.

It was known by Air Survey that the Germans were using Fuka landing ground on the coast several miles west of el Daba and for that reason it was not destroyed because if Rommel was to be sent back to Egypt he would almost certainly land there. (And, ideed, he did). Surely Auchinleck or Gott would have asked Stirling to have a patrol handy nearby in case some high-ranking German (Kesselring, Rommel) flew in to take charge of the leaderless Germans. An attempt to capture such a figure should have been a LRDG priority, but such ventures did not figure in Montgomery's pedestrian plan.

The 7th Armoured Division could not attempt any such romantic foray because they had been scheduled to contain the mighty 21st Panzer Division during the early days of Montgomery's battle. But why not use the 4th Indian Division? Ah, but Montgomery was not keen to offer glory to the elite Indian Army. They were held in check, and there were murmurs at the front about Montgomery's almost derisory treatment of the famous Indian Division.

Everyone was tired and emotionally shattered on the morning of October 24th.

Where was the plan for a sweep behind the equally exhausted but numerically inferior enemy?

The Official History of the Second World War said (referring to Alamein) that, 'little happened on the ground during the 24th October'. What an indictment of Montgomery's Master Plan! If the full facts had been known then to Wavell and Auchinleck banished to India how they would have fumed! Surely the fact that so many lives had been lost and so little gained must have made poor Gott turn in his grave.

And there were men with Montgomery at Alamein who knew the desert so well.

Freyberg, for example.

It would have been a nice gesture to the Empire to put Lt.-General Sir Bernard Freyberg in charge after Gott's tragic death. Churchill was known to hold Bernard Freyberg, VC and triple DSO, hero of the Dardanelles, in the highest regard, referring to him as 'the Salamander' after the mythical creature which could live in fire. Freyberg knew the desert, and there he was on the night of October 23rd in the midst of Montgomery's murderous fire. What would Freyberg be thinking now? Surely he would be expecting some flanking movement. That was the whole idea of the Alamein Ambush.

In the postwar interview with Barrie Pitt when Montgomery referred to Auchinleck as, 'Too political! Too much Indian Army!' he was asked about Bernard Freyberg and the reply was equally dismissive. 'Freyberg? Useless! Block of stone for a head!' Might one suggest that of the two it was Montgomery who had a 'block of stone for a head!'

Montgomery called his October 23rd advance Operation LIGHTFOOT. It turned out to be anything but lightfooted!

There is nothing like being bombed for stiffening the resolve and even though the Germans were leaderless their *esprit de corps* united them to an opposition so fierce Montgomery's Plan was thrown off course.

Not all saw merit in Montgomery.

There was General 'Gertie' Tuker of the 4th Indian Division, described by historian Ronald Lewin as 'one of the wisest of all British divisional commanders' and who was never afraid to recommend withdrawal if it saved a massacre and offered the opportunity to regroup and attack under more favourable circumstances. His 4th Indian Division was a tiptop infantry unit by any standards and Tuker preached, 'if the "approach to battle" is wrong the battle itself will not be right'. The 4th Indian must have been straining at the bit, isolated in the middle of the Alamein Line and waiting, waiting, waiting for some imaginative instruction on the morning of October 24th. The Miteiriyeh Ridge should have been by-passed. The Maginot Line was. The Germans did not advance dead body over dead body. They by-passed the Maginot Line and swept into France. This was World War Two, not 1914–18!

Lt.-General Sir Francis Tuker had been at the staff college, Camberley, and had gone into the Indian Army. There was often a lack of rapport between British officers in the Indian Army and those serving in British service. Brian Montgomery asserts that the fact that his brother had failed to be accepted by the Indian Army had left its mark, 'a view I hold with reluctance', but Brian's belief does explain Bernard Montgomery's attitude towards the Indian Army. Many questions were asked why Montgomery did not employ the 4th Indian Division in the eventual pursuit of the Axis forces on November 6th 1942.

General Messervey who had commanded the Indian Division against Rommel while serving under both Wavell and Auchinleck was also treated in calvalier manner by the unappreciative Montgomery.

General Morshead, Austalian Commander, was a 'desert commander' to his fingertips. When, a few days after October 23rd General Horrocks complimented Morshead on the extreme bravery and the success of the Australian 9th Division the reply was typically laid back, "Oh, the boys were interested!", a classic understatement.

It might be helpful to readers to understand my very strong views if I mention the aspect under which I surveyed the three Battles of the Desert.

For the Wavell season I was at RAF Intelligence HQ, Cairo, studying

MASSACRE AT ALAMEIN?

strips of air survey photos and drawing target maps. I thus saw the 1940/41 battle from a sort of 'bird's eye view'.

For the Auchinleck season I was on the ground, going forward in the desert at the end of 1941 and retreating in the early months of 1942.

For the Montgomery season I was with a South African Survey Company stationed at Maadi, just outside Cairo, doing the same 'bird's eye view' work from the latest strips of air photos and intelligence reports.

There was however a difference between the Wavell and Auchinleck seasons and the Montgomery season.

During 1940/41 I had been surrounded by the keen interest of the RAF Intelligence Section personnel.

During 1941/42 I had been surrounded by the actual fighting forces on the ground and, obviously, the interest had been especially keen, and exciting.

However, during the 1942/43 period under Montgomery I was surrounded by the South African influence and I found this to be quite different from that of other members of the Empire; Australia, New Zealand, and Indian in particular.

Those three countries were 'excitedly involved' in the events going on in the desert. The South Africans were 'judicially involved'.

Unlike the other Empire countries, who seemed to be fully committed to the war, the South Africans although committed had reservations. Perhaps that was because they were the one country which belonged to Africa and were therefore fighting 'at home' whereas the rest of the Allies were fighting 'away'.

There were also questions about their efforts in the desert. During the first siege of Tobruk a South African Brigade was expected to arrive at Bir el Gubbi but it never appeared. Lewin, writing of the efficiency of the 8th Army field artillery added a sting in the tail when praising the South Africans: 'even the South Africans, *who were not otherwise notably effective,* did great execution.' When Tobruk fell to Rommel it was General Klopper of the South Africans who surrendered to Rommel, June 20, 1942, and although the Australians could not have done any better there remained a certain stigma in the fact that the South Africans lost what the Australians had held. The fall of Tobruk so pleased Hitler

131

that Rommel was promoted to field marshal.

This judging of every move made in the desert sharpened my own observation from the details extracted from the strips of air photos sent in by the RAF for target map reproduction.

Had everyone's observation and criticism of Montgomery been as acute as the South Africans he may well have had his wings clipped before he carried on with the excessive loss of life.

Rommel had no respect for Montgomery as a tactician, whereas he was quick to praise Wavell, Auchinleck, and the LRDG patrols. It is from German reports that we learn that in 1943 General Alexander did control Montgomery to a certain extent, but by then Montgomery was the Victor of Alamein, and a winner is all too often forgiven the rough means employed in victory. Victory is success, and nothing succeeds like success! Churchill wanted a national hero and he was determind to create one. Montgomery, who had got on in life by a privilege of birth and a formidable mother, was the lucky beneficiary of Churchill's largesse.

The South Africans reckoned that they had received an undeserved bad press and were rather upset about this so it led them to judge carefully every move made in the desert battle, and this acutely sharpened my own observation and assessment of what was happening. I was the only one in that South African target map drawing office who had been in the western desert and I was frequently asked to look at this or that strip of air photos to see if I recognised the various areas. Having roamed the desert navigating Derek Rawnsley's RAF Intelligence Patrol there was little of that vast area I had not seen or been close to. My standing was further enhanced when I said I had spoken to General Auchinleck (albeit dressed simply by a towel round my waist) and that I knew well Montgomery's brother, Colin Roger, our unpopular vicar in Wallasey.

It became fascinating in an eerie kind of way because we could see the action but take no part. We saw some photos taken a mere twentyfour hours previous. Altogether these photos told a slightly different story to the one being put out by the newspapers. Reports from Alamein were, of course, censored by Montgomery.

The enemy has suffered heavy losses. We are advancing steadily. Victory will be ours!

Who would worry with news like that?

Because of this special Springbok interest we soon found out what the South Africans had been asked to do on the night of October 23rd.

It was to capture part of the Miteiriya Ridge, ten miles in from the coast.

Our later and considered reaction to that was to wonder why the South Africans were not joined by the nearby 4th Indian Division and told to by-pass the Miteiriya Ridge by a broad sweep in the south and get behind that ridge and possibly the next objective too, Kidney Ridge. Montgomery had given the enemy seven weeks to mine this area so that made it more difficult but it was a better plan to by-pass than to cling to this 'Charge and occupy Hill Sixty!' World War One attitude.

Two brigades of the 1st South African Division set off that night to occupy that fateful ridge. Engaged in this operation were the 1st Battalion of the Durban Light Infantry, the Imperial Light Horse, and the Rand Light Infantry. When the terrific barrage opened (heard in Alexandria sixty miles away) the Rand Light Infantry moved forward and with the Durbans close behind they made an opening charge of nearly half a mile before barbed wire, close enemy fire and mines halted their progress, and there was some bayonet charging and hand to hand fighting. The South Africans succeeded in the objective they had been given and an agreed 'success signal' was fired to register this with the adjacent groups.

That was the end of the success story because the Germans became alerted to the attack and many of the Durbans in the rear were cut down before they could join the advance. The Durbans who survived and bravely charged forward came across Axis minefields not charted by Montgomery's Intelligence. They were joined by the Imperial Light Horse and there were bloody close-range bayonet skirmishes, man to man, South African versus German. Italian fire was then directed at the South Africans and the advance was halted shortly after midnight and the operation was well behind the timing set by Montgomery.

The 2nd Brigade also blundered into strongly held enemy positions not charted and as a result Montgomery's opening barrage had not directed any fire into that area to clear the way for the South Africans and the steadfast Germans met the South African advance with heavy mortar and machine gun fire causing heavy losses to the Springboks. So tremendous had been the unexpected opposition the battalions of the 2nd Brigade failed to reach their objective.

The 3rd Brigade was also bogged down and, well behind schedule, could not move forward until almost 3 o'clock in the morning. By now there was serious conjestion, the unfortunate Durbans once again suffering heavy losses. Those of the Durbans still alive gathered together and charged in once more, chanting war songs of the Zulu tribes and meeting heavy machine gun fire with rifle fire and bayonet, and struggling over barbed wire entanglements. Their short rushes, pauses, and rushes repeated, were joined by remnants from other groups and eventually, against all the odds, the 3rd Company reached its objective.

Losses had been much heavier than anticipated but the attacks had been of the bravest and the South Africans were in no mood for an unfair press this time.

In the early hours of the morning a Durban transport platoon arrived with a hot breakfast for each man. There was plenty to spare. So many who had set out on the 23rd at 21.40 hours no longer were able to partake of breakfast. The Durbans alone had lost a quarter of their men in that one night.

Just as the Scots remembered the sound of bagpipes over the sands of Alamein so in their eventual letters home did the Springboks remember the traditional hymn of the South African Division, 'Abide With Me', played by their regimental bugler in remembrance of those who had just died.

What Montgomery had called his 'crumbling' operation was going to be very expensive in troop losses and the commanding officers in the field wondered if he would shift his attention to the south and order a major advance from there rather than along the coast. It was believed by many that this would be the sort of move which Auchinleck or Gott would have emphasised from the very start. This method, adopted by Wavell, Auchinleck, Gott, and Rommel, and also recommended by Graziani, was to open with a bombardment which demanded attention from the enemy, and next would be a three-pronged attack below and around the main enemy positions with the object of surrounding the enemy who would then 'have no place to go'. This was a plan peculiar to desert warfare, and it worked, as the five generals mentioned could testify. Was Montgomery going to be 'dangerously different' just to pig-headedly be different from the other desert generals?

Did he fear that unless he was 'different' his victory would be likened to doing merely what Auchinleck or Gott would have done?

On the morning of October 24th Montgomery could see that His Plan had not gone as hoped for. At the northern (coastal) end XXX Corps infantry divisions had moved towards the Miteiriya Ridge (about ten miles inland). The divisions included the 9th Australians, 51st Highland, 2nd New Zealand, and 1st South African, and they had attacked in line. Each division reported the same as the South Africans, namely, that early success had met with stiffening resistance and final impasse in a murderous 'traffic jam'.

Not sufficient gaps had been made in the minefields for the follow-up tanks to advance. And remember, when Rommel arrived at Alamein he had no minefields. Montgomery's delay had given the Germans time to lay these murderous fields. And also bear in mind, at this juncture Montgomery was not fighting Rommel, the German hero was still in Germany.

Further south XIII Corps had attempted a diversionary attack (instead of a Desert-Rat-like 'determined sweep') which had become bogged down by the 21st Panzers. However, the Germans gathered the scattered Panzer groups together and headed north, leaving an Axis 'Southern group' to further defend the Miteiriya Ridge. The 15th Panzers had suffered heavy losses and the remnants fought to join hands with the 21st Panzers and thus form a resolute defence unit to face further Allied attacks. Rommel had left such an order, that his Panzers should consolidate and not become small units to be picked off one at a time by the enemy.

During the afternoon heavy fighting continued with the 1st Armoured Division battling furiously but making little headway against determined enemy resistance, organised by von Thoma and the other generals who had been left behind by Rommel.

In the absence of Rommel and his Chief of Staff Bayerlein and now with the death of Stumme it was left to von Thoma to organise the

MASSACRE AT ALAMEIN?

German/Italian resistance and this he did with typical German thoroughness. He must have guessed (or perhaps his Intelligence informed him) that Montgomery was not going to employ the obvious desert tactic of a determined sweep from the south and so the Axis forces massed in the north for whatever the second night, October 24/25th, held for the front line troops.

The British troops not actually fighting that morning, tired though they were from lack of sleep, were ordered to 'dig in' and the infantry remained in those dugouts during the heat of the day.

Already the British had collected many prisoners-of-war (POWs) and they were shepherded east towards temporary POW camps between Alamein and Alexandria.

Many troops, writing home later, wrote of the heavy congestion of forces and vehicles which the dawn light exposed. The area made an easy target for enemy shelling. Congestion of troops like the Allies were suffering now was virtually a crime in the vast space the desert offered.

One man wrote, 'there seemed to be miles and miles of nothing but our army'.

Dispersal and speed are life-saving elements in the desert but it was the morning speed of action by the enemy which surprised and dismayed the Allies. It really shook the troops when the Germans hit back first thing in the morning.

But there you are; von Thoma was a more experienced desert fighter than Montgomery and the German general hit back when all Montgomery's men wanted to do was have breakfast, take stock, lick their wounds, and prepare themselves for the next move in the Montgomery Plan.

The German Stuka planes swept in, dive bombing the forward troops despite the fact that the Germans were supposed to have 'only a handful' of planes. They were causing panic with the few they did have. As many as thirty Stuka raids were made on the luckless 68th Medium Regiment that day. The RAF hit back, so there was quite a lot of air activity.

The front line troops waited for the night with fearful trepidation. Last night had been Hell. Death was on a knife edge. Each man wondered, 'Will I be alive tomorrow?'

The 7th Armoured Division (I was told later, socialising in Cairo) would have loved to join forces with the Free French Brigade, the 50th and/or the 44th Division and especially the 4th Indian Division (in their opinion 'wasting time' defending the isolated Ruweisat Ridge which was central and back of the Alamein Line), and make a determined and speedy drive to arrive at el Daba on the coast, *behind* the enemy, thus ambushing him.

Nothing so imaginative or speedy (or othodox for the desert) had been planned. General Harding's orders from Montgomery were for the famous 7th Armoured Division to hold their position in the south. This gave the men a feeling that they had been relegated to 'the Cinderella' (General Harding's term) of the party. The magnificent 7th had to contain the 21st Panzer (who were soon moved north by von Thoma) during the early hours of the battle. The 7th were then to swing west and north towards el Daba when they had penetrated various minefields, hold a ridge known as Himeimat, and not lose too many men because the 7th would be required as a full-strength unit in 'a few days time'! General Harding later wrote that his problem was to carry out these tasks without getting into a skirmish with the enemy and so lose men and thus become a unit below strength. Montgomery wanted them at full strength for future use in his plan. But, was Montgomery being too slow? Should it not have been 'immediate use', this planned drive towards el Daba on the coast and behind von Thoma's main army? Why 'penetrate' the minefields? Why not go round them?

In November 1941 Auchinleck had found that his starting line of a couple of miles was too narrow and his large army had soon become congested when the initial attack began. His Alamein Line of between 30 and 35 miles gave him the opportunity to spread his front line troops so that each had its own space, and could move at its own speed. Desert veterans also knew that the groups at the northern end (on the coast) would meet different weather conditions to those in the south (desert conditons).

The coastal strip of the southern Med. has all the vagaries of coastal weather almost anywhere in the world: rain, shine, gale-force winds, storms, lightning, calm, and so on . . . most unpredictable.

Inland the desert has more settled weather: 120 degrees by day and 80 by night, an alteration in temperature which produces the dawn dew which

137

MASSACRE AT ALAMEIN?

gives plants, shrubs, grasses their daily life-supporting drink, and which skilled desert-dwellers make use of with several ingenious water-saving devices and so on . . . .. very predictable weather.

The dependable weather of the desert is only disrupted by the occasional Khamseen. The predictable weather helps planning. The unpredictability of the coastal weather can be disruptive when set plans are put into operation, as Auchinleck and Rommel found out in November and December of 1941.

When I spoke with fellow-servicemen in Cairo who had been in the desert during the Auchinleck advance and retreat one thing which surprised me was the complaint about difficulties caused by rapidly changing weather conditions. Inland with Derek Rawnsley's patrol we found the desert weather to be constant and it caused no problem to our planned movements. The exception, of course, was when we got caught in a sandstorm and then everything sits still in the desert until the storm blows away, usually about an hour or two.

Did Montgomery have this understanding and 'feeling' for the desert? He had never spent time 'in the blue' and he was not the kind of man to listen to those who had. Was he aware, for example, that the Free French in the south of the Alamein Line might have different weather to the Australians in the north?

There were many who began to feel a little uneasy. Did Montgomery know what he was doing with his 'We'll knock 'em for six!' philosophy?

One wonders if Montgomery knew, or even wanted to know, about the chivalrous 'Rules of Combat' built up between the Commonwealth Forces and the Axis Forces. These rules were humane and were peculiar to desert warfare, but they did nothing to lessen the fierceness and dedicated integrity of the fighting while opposing forces were actually in combat.

There are dozens of authenticated cases of this special humane gentlemanly Chivalry which took place in the desert. This meant that POWs played the game and an observer could come across a group of, say, a hundred POWs sitting quietly on the sand waiting to be fed, and guarded by a couple of soldiers armed only with a rifle.

This desert code enabled the sick to be attended to by the nearest doctor or medical centre once the battle had been settled.

MASSACRE AT ALAMEIN?

At Mersa Metruh's hospital it might have astonished Montgomery to see injured British, German, Commonwealth, French and Italian soldiers and airmen sharing the same wards and attended to by an 'international' team of doctors and nurses. When Rommel overtook Mersa Matruh in June 1942 he insisted on entering the hospital to shake hands with every doctor and nurse and to assure patients that they would be quite safe as the battle passed them by. Rommel asked British doctors to carry on for a few weeks until his own doctors arrived and the British doctors would not then be taken prisoner but would be escorted to neutral Switzerland.

In May 1942 the fighting around Gazala was particularly fierce but one report tells of a German vehicle displaying a white flag drawing up at a British medical centre. Inside the centre were some injured Axis troops. From the German car stepped a young officer who offered medical supplies to be used for both Axis and Allied patients. The Chief MO accepted the supplies, saw that the German officer and his driver had a hot meal, and watched as they drove back to their own lines.

A few weeks after this incident the advancing Germans came across a group of badly wounded British soldiers being attended to by an NCO. A German officer stopped his car, jumped out and offered the British NCO bandages and other medical supplies. The NCO saluted the German officer who returned the salute, wished the injured well, and drove off.

The water holes were never poisoned (certainly not to my knowledge. Booby traps, yes, but I did not hear of any poisoning of the water) as the troops moved backwards and forwards. The booby traps included: whistles which exploded when blown, pens which blew up when collected from the sandy floor, but other than these minor Italian 'toys' which did not seem to fool anyone because there were warnings given, the danger was restricted to organised minefields which opposing sappers were expected to clear for their own troops to move forward safely. Troops were always careful on entering deserted buildings because these might be booby-trapped. However, I personally saw countless deserted buildings but not one which was booby-trapped. After all, the advancing troops might want these buildings during an enforced withdrawal.

German and Italian POWs arriving in Alexandria, Cairo, or other POW camps were able to retain their dignity because there was no attempt to humiliate or humble them. Victors did not boast or strut. Prisoners had been captured in noble combat and deserved to be treated with respect.

This humane understanding was something which the desert fighters on each side had come to understand, share, and appreciate.

British and Commonwealth troops injured during the October 23/24th night fighting were treated by the RAMC who had the 2nd, 7th, 14th and 15th Light Field Ambulance Companies, and they also treated German and Italians who had injuries. These prisoners were then sent to a rear POW camp.

While in Germany that October Rommel secretly reported that most of his tanks were decrepit and barely fit for action, and of the Alam Halfa battle he claimed that the British were able to fire ten shells for every one of his.

Alamein was always a battle the British were going to win; unless something dramatic or utterly stupid took place.

And so to the second night of the Montgomery Plan.

It was with misgivings that most of the Empire Forces surveyed the situation.

The conjestion was terrifying in its density.

South Africans, New Zealanders, Australians, and Indians lived in countries where there was 'space'. They would travel a hundred miles to have dinner with friends, or fifty-plus to visit a theatre. That was why they took so easily to desert warfare and especially to the long-range raids made by the patrols.

English people lived in densely populated towns; children played with children who lived in the same street, there was a pub on one corner and a shop on another. A church and a cinema and a fish-and-chip shop existed within a radius of a couple of hundred yards, and should there be a river the people on one side rarely crossed to mingle with people on the other side. Everything was packed together; close at hand.

That is how it was at Alamein; packed together.

The very thing Auchinleck, having learnt from experience, wanted to avoid.

The Germans and Italians had congregated in the north of the Alamein Line. They numbered less than half of Montgomery's front line army.

MASSACRE AT ALAMEIN?

'Keep with the herd!' is a rule of survival in the jungle so Rommel's order to his Panzers had been that when Montgomery attacked the Panzers should close ranks to form a solid unit. A loner who strayed from the herd would soon be picked off by the predator.

The Battle of Alamein, 24/25th October, looked like being a face-to-face close encounter, 'unit' killing 'unit', the team with the most 'units' being the winners of this murderous war game.

Montgomery was very 'English' in his concentration of numbers. Auchinleck had thought in terms of a wider horizon, working closely with his 'second army' of LRDG and SAS. This breadth of vision appealed to the Empire Forces.

Montgomery's forces were so packed together that the enemy fire (accurate in any circumstance) had little difficulty in finding targets.

The word went round that the senior officers were coming to the front line to review the situation, but there was a feeling that anything they might think would not be listened to by the 'This is My Plan' General Montgomery. The plan that night would be to press on through the minefields, Rommel's 'Devil's Garden!'

And so it turned out.

The British Forces found it ever more difficult to penetrate the enemy minefields, especially in the face of accurate and determined enemy fire. Nerves began to break and General Harding later reported that one such man who cracked was one of his sergeants from 'C Gun' group who went raving mad and had to be led away. Harding also wrote of his anxiety at that time of the danger from the confusion of 'loss of direction' caused by the terrible nerve-shattering noise, the traffic jams, the slowness of movement, the fear of the minefields underfoot, machine-gun bullets ahead, and shells falling from above. There was not a moment when the nerves could relax and the mind pause to take stock. The infantry was pinned to the ground. The tanks were being picked off one by burning one.

Montgomery's weeks of 'intense training' (without enemy fire to interrupt) was only partially of value under the pressure the enemy was now exerting. Had Montgomery allowed for the effect of this pressure? What his men had tried in practice was not possible in that terrible conjestion which faced the infantry and the tanks.

MASSACRE AT ALAMEIN?

Losses were becoming alarmingly high.

And for what?

There was precious little advance possible in the north. Why not in the south? The predictable expected south? For God's sake, surely it made sense now to move in the south! The Free French in the south had advanced but had to halt because of 'The Plan'.

General Harding recalled that he remembered vividly the long snake-like lines of tanks, guns, and vehicles 'exploding one by one' with burning and dying men flinging themselves out. "I could not risk further losses. My instructions were to keep my division intact!" O.K., but please tell that to the Germans!

The strongest weapon the Germans had at Alamein on the night of 24/25th was the heavy gun, far more in number than Montgomery had at the front, and the heavy guns were used to devastating effect. Eventually, of course, the German guns would run out of ammunition because despite lack of encouragement and support from Montgomery the LRDG and SAS patrols had taken it upon themselves to curtail the German line of supplies from the west by frequently raiding the convoys and dumps.

That second terrible night, with men dying by the hundred and no real advantage in ground being gained, the field commanders pondered anxiously: should the slaughter continue, or should the men halt, regroup, and use their numerical superiority in a more open-flanked and daylight advance, when everyone could see what was going on?

Montgomery was known to be keen on night fighting, but that had been on exercise in England. Perhaps the moment had arrived to re-think the Alamein Plan. Attack on a wider front. The present conjestion was not only lethal but, if anything, it was to the advantage of the Axis. Had Rommel produced some clever trick of psychology to make Montgomery stick doggedly to the north? A wider approach would stretch the limited resources of the Axis and thus lessen the numbers in the various groups making them easier to pick off one by one. The British would benefit from a wider front because each section would have more space, and space was something the desert had plenty of to offer. Auchinleck had made provision for this in his own plan, and, surely, a determined sweep from the south was crying out to be put into operation.

MASSACRE AT ALAMEIN?

The deadly sands of Alamein continued to claim their haul of blood, bodies and chaos, minute by relentless minute.

The commanders decided to put the position to Montgomery, but, where was he?

They found the Chief of Staff, Freddy de Guingand.

It was half past three in the morning. The noise was deafening.

"Where is Montgomery?" the generals asked.

"He's asleep," Freddy replied, "he went to bed at his usual time!"

The generals hid their astonishment, and held in check whatever their private feelings were.

"We must see him. Things are not going to plan."

Montgomery was wakened and the position was put to him. If the fighting went on as it was the infantry would be decimated, and soon there would be no tanks and tank crews left. "Wouldn't it be better if . . ."

Sir Brian Horrocks records Montgomery's chilling reply.

"I am prepared, if necessary, to lose one hundred per cent casualties in tanks!"

Anyone requiring confirmation of that should read, for example, the article by Sir Brian Horrocks in the *News of The World* May 7th 1967.

That was it. Montgomery had no alternative plan.

When Montgomery arrived in the desert it was not the 8th Army which was 'unready', it was Montgomery. Montgomery the Unready. He needed time to review the situation. He needed time to get his breath, find his feet, get the feel of the sand between his toes. Get his knees brown. Auchinleck had spent eight months setting up Alamein and had then been brutally treated by an impatient Churchill. However, if Montgomery simply continued with the Auchinleck Plan, as Gott would have done, then laurels for the victory would not entirely be credited to Montgomery. It would, therefore, be to Montgomery's personal ambition-wise advantage to let a couple of months pass. Let the memory of Auchinleck pass. Let new troops and new commanders arrive. Publicity. That was what Montgomery needed. Publicity. 'My Plan', No more retreat! Wait until we have everything ready (never mind that 'time' also gave the enemy the opportunity to recover from losing the second Battle of Alamein).

Philip Warner, writing a mini-biography of Auchinleck and referring to

MASSACRE AT ALAMEIN?

Montgomery, declared that Bernard Montgomery became so besotted with his own grandeur that he was not able to contemplate any general, British or American, as his equal. Also mentioned is the claim that Montgomery was not above accepting the work of others as if it were his own.

So, on the afternoon of October 25th 'The Plan' continued but eventually by the evening even Montgomery could see the futility of pushing forward inch by inch into the minefields and enemy fire in the Miteiriya Ridge area and, would you believe it!, he ordered the angle of his attack NORTHWARDS!, into the already gridlocked Hell of that bloodbath which the South Africans, New Zealanders, Australians and British were struggling.

In the south the Free French had not been too heavily mauled and their losses had been slight and they held their objective, the Himeimat Ridge. But, there was no order for a rapid flanking movement. On the 25th October the southern troops were still in position. The opportunity of an early first or second day massed raid towards el Daba (where Rommel's Chief of Staff's men were stationed) had gone.

That night the attack by General Harding's 7th Armoured Division made little progress and, obeying orders not to lose too many men because Montgomery wanted to be able to call on a full-strength unit to hurl into battle in due course, Harding made no further attempt to break through the enemy lines.

(Later in the battle General Harding was seriously wounded when his tank was hit and later still, as Field Marshal Harding, he died in England from his injuries.)

On the afternoon of 25th October the 4/8 Hussars were ordered to advance north-west to support the 50th Division who were in a central position on the Alamein Line. Tanks were exploding and burning too easily, partly because most tanks used aero high-octane fuel which would ignite on contact when hit by a red-hot shell or bullet and thus blow the tank to bits either killing the crew outright or roasting them to death. Many tank crews said that in desert warfare they would have felt safer in armoured vehicles, like those used by the LRDG.

The pattern of the battle continued unchanged.

In London Churchill was already preparing for the church bells to ring

MASSACRE AT ALAMEIN?

to signal a famous victory at Alamein, despite the ominous fact that many observers in London proclaimed themselves to be 'very worried' by Montgomery's slow progress. Churchill was not worried. Maybe he said to himself that, surely Alamein was a battle even Montgomery could not lose!

In Berlin Hitler was alarmed by the news from the desert. Where was Rommel? He was in a rest home near Vienna! Hitler was furious.

Rommel was immediately despatched back to the desert, arriving at Fuka the arrival point as expected by British Intelligence, on October 25th . . . but . . . where was Montgomery's 'reception committee'? Why oh why did you not co-operate more closely with the LRDG? Why were you so rude to David Stirling?

Hitler was insanely furious over this desert fiasco. Failure of any kind was the last thing he wanted at that time. He seemed to be getting nowhere in Russia. Rommel must remain a national hero. If the Panzerarmee was to be beaten in the desert it must go down gloriously fighting to the last man. It would then look good to the German people: 100,000 Axis soldiers, of which more than half were 'inferior' Italians, holding out against 200,000-plus Allied troops who also had that many men in reserve, plus the fact that the enemy (Germany's) had hundreds more tanks to fall back on. Only the genius of Rommel was halting the British hordes! Goebbels' propaganda would have to make the position look good.

Hitler despatched an order that the Germans must fight to the last man. Victory or Death! Heil Hitler!

Montgomery had declared that he would fight to the last member of his tank crews. Victory or Death! Heil Montgomery!

Do you think that fair comment or not?

Is it a scenario for a massacre?

Have Hitler and Montgomery between them set the scene for nothing more than a face-saving bloodbath?

Those of us at the South African Survey Unit at Maadi did wonder, on examining air photos and reading the latest reports, if Montgomery was using Desert Rats as cannon fodder like the Old Contemptibles on the Somme. Where was the flanking movement? Why was everybody confined into a tiny area? There was space in the desert, why not use it?

Montgomery retired to his caravan every night at 21.30 hours, justifying his isolationism by casting scorn on Rommel's availability... 'he is always with his troops. That is not the way to pursue high command!'

That view is, of course, debatable.

From the night of 25/26th October onwards the gallant Australians in the north of the Line fought their way inch by inch over a period of nine days after which Montgomery's sheer weight of numbers began to inexorably take effect.

Clinging to the north like filings to a static magnet the name LIGHTFOOT seemed inappropriate for the sluggish and murderous operation in hand so a new name was created to give the impression of a change in strategy. Operation SUPERCHARGE . . . although 'charge' was hardly a suitable description of progress considering it consisted mainly of night attacks through minefields; a slow plodding killing movement. Montgomery seemed more afraid of Rommel's reputation than of Rommel's ever-diminishing army. And now the great Teutonic hero was here in person! Montgomery seemed afraid to take the slightest chance. Keep plodding. Men might die but if he plodded on he could not do otherwise than win.

It did not take Rommel long to realise that Montgomery was 'attack along the coast' conscious and that suited Rommel because he did not have the manpower to face a fierce swift sweep from the south. At the Qattara end (known to Egyptians as Munkhafad al Qattara) the Allies were poised, ready and waiting, and as long as they stayed there it suited Rommel perfectly. Montgomery was effectively destroying the ambush situation which Auchinleck had so cunningly lured Rommel into.

Rommel must have been a little surprised that there was no 'Reception Committee' waiting for him at Fuka when he arrived. It was the third day of the battle. What had happened to the imaginative LRDG and SAS? Why hadn't they been sent by Montgomery to capture Rommel?, a raid on the brave and adventurous lines of that led by Lt.-Col. Geoffrey Keyes, VC, at Beda Littoria almost a year ago (17/18 November 1941) and, sadly for the British, at a time when Rommel had been on a flying visit to Athens. Montgomery had no such 'Capture Rommel Dead or Alive'plan at Fuka. There are many who believe that General Gott would have 'done an

MASSACRE AT ALAMEIN?

Auchinleck' and had a go at capturing the 'Desert Fox'. That was something Montgomery never succeeded in doing. Rommel eluded him all the way out of the desert until the inevitable Axis surrender on May 13th 1943. Seven months, and in all that time Montgomery failed to capture Germany's national hero, Field Marshal Erwin Rommel.

On October 27th Rommel, although he knew that barring a miracle the British would sooner or later win at Alamein, tried a determined raid through what he considered to be a weak link in the Alamein Line, south of the Australian sector and near to Kidney Ridge. It was something of a suicide attempt: bold, imaginative, and with a possible valuable prize in the shape of support from the Egyptians and the Egyptian Army. If only he could reach Alexandria! What a hysterical uprising that would create! His Intelligence gave Rommel confirmation that lighted windows would be used at Farouk's Ras el Tin palace at the edge of the breakwater of Alexandria's West Harbour (and romantically near the site of the ancient Pharos Lighthouse, one of the Seven Wonders of the World) and Montaza Palace at the other side of Alexandria Bay as a guide for German submarines.

Rommel still had the map he had drawn for the Alam Halfa battle and it contained routes for raids not only on Alexandria but also on Cairo which, if successful, the Egyptian Army would co-operate with.

His imaginative foray on October 27th failed. He had already lost far too many tanks and he was hopelessly outnumbered so, short of ammunition and fuel, he had to return to his position west of the Alamein Line. But that is what desert war is all about, making use of the space which is abundantly available, avoiding the deadly traffic jams which happened in the bloody fields of Flanders! and, dare one say it?, in the bloody sands at the conjested north of the Alamein Line!

Lieutenant Berndt was Goebbel's 'man in the desert' and he acted as Rommel's 'publicity agent', and Berndt alerted Goebbels to the inevitability of a German defeat in the desert so that Goebbels could organise German propaganda accordingly.

An entry in the Panzerarmee War Diary stated that if an expected tanker did not arrive on October 26th there would be a fuel crisis. That day the *Proserpina* with 3000 tons of fuel and the *Tergestea* with 1000 tons were sunk. That really did mean that Rommel was sunk and that he was 'mafeesh benzine'. His men could not have reached Alexandria even if they had broken through the Alamein Line.

On November 3rd Berndt flew to Berlin to break the news to a furious Adolf Hitler who sent Kesselring to the desert on November 4th with a confirmation of the order, 'Victory or Death!' "*The situation demands that the positions at el Alamein be held to the last man. A retreat is out of the question. Victory or Death! Heil Hitler!*" and the message bore Hitler's personal signature. Rommel could not treat it as non-existent.

Hitler's virtual 'death sentence' to Rommel and the Panzerarmee found Rommel torn between duty and conscience. He could see that Montgomery's commanders were having the same moral problem. It seemed to many observers that neither Hitler nor Montgomery had any humanitarian considerations.

Rommel, unlike the sleeping Montgomery, stayed up and watched the crazy noisy firework display which despite its intensity was gaining little or no advancement for the British general. Rommel wrote to his wife that he was unable to sleep because of the carnage. He was trapped if he stood his ground. Another fuel tanker, the *Louisiana*, had been sunk. He had enough fuel to fall back to Fuka, but, there was Hitler's 'Death Sentence', to stand and fight!

On November 3rd the 4th South Africans reported by wireless that they had broken through and were standing by.

The Germans were astonished that Montgomery did not drive home his many advantages and so bring the massacre to an honourable conclusion.

On November 4th it is recorded that Rommel did not have a single operational tank available. General Ritter (Ritter means 'Knight') von Thoma was still fighting alongside his men at the front line even though the continued fighting meant nothing but more dead. For him it really was Victory or Death! Anyone other than Montgomery would have seen that the moment had arrived to surround the enemy who would have been forced to surrender. Montgomery knew exactly what was going on because he had the advantage of impeccable Intelligence information from the highly secret 'Ultra' sources with their fast intercept and decoding service.

Kesselring, November 4th, could not sanction Rommel disobeying

MASSACRE AT ALAMEIN?

Captured General von Thoma surrenders to General Montgomery

MASSACRE AT ALAMEIN?

Hitler's order and when he left to fly back to Germany it was with an open-ended, "I'll leave it to you!", comment that he gave Rommel.

When von Thoma asked Rommel about stopping the bloodbath the field marshal's reply was the same as Kesselring's comment, "I'll leave it to you!" Unfortunately von Thoma left it a bit too late and was captured.

One man Montgomery did work closely with was Air Marshal Tedder (both became members of The Savage Club) and the Allied superiority in the air should have shortened the number of days Montgomery was bogged down at Alamein. However, he did not seem to have the imagination to see further than a few yards in front of his nose.

November 5th. To the British that date is forever Firework Night. To those at Alamein it is certain that they never wanted to see or hear another firework as long as they lived. 'Remember, remember, the Fifth of November!' November 5th was also significant to Rommel.

It was his birthday.

Erwin Rommel was born at Heidenheim in Wurttemberg on November 5th 1891. He served with the Wurttemberg Mountain Battalion in World War One and took part in the war against the Italians, and was decorated for bravery.

On the eve of November 5th several decisions were made which led to the German retreat and the British advance, so technically the battle was over. But who was responsible? It seems that there was a general mood that 'enough is enough' and that mood, pervading the whole of the Alamein area, was the real cause for the stopping of further slaughter.

For example: on the night of November 4th Rommel decided that enough was enough and defied Hitler's Death or Victory order by retreating towards el Daba on November 5th. The Australians finally broke through in the north and without waiting for explicit orders to advance they pressed on regardless. In the south the stationary Free French had also had enough and they pushed forward and made considerable advance which was much more than a mere break-through. Things were at last moving. But, can it be put down to one man? Most observers at the time believed that it was a combination of several things and not due to any genius by Montgomery. It *had* to happen. Sheer weight of superiority by the Allies made this so, and the overall desperation that 'enough is enough'

MASSACRE AT ALAMEIN?

shared by the Panzerarmee, the Free French in the south and the Australians in the north finally got things moving. The break-out was on. Forward at last.

Once the German retreat was firmly established Hitler extricated himself from the position of having his orders broken by ordering Rommel to 'retreat if necessary', something which of course Rommel was already doing. Had Rommel waited for this order there would have been no troops left to make a retreat.

Once again Montgomery was slow to follow up.

A sandstorm on November 5th made it difficult for anyone to reinforce the Free French advance in the south and by the time Montgomery get cracking in the north Rommel was on his way, the weather on the coast coming to his rescue like Fortune favouring the brave! The Rommel diaries record, 'only the rain on 6th and 7th November saved us from annihilation', and the slowing down by the hesitant Montgomery of the British advance starting on the morning of November 5th.

Thousands had died in that small conjested area around Alamein. Had there been an alternative? Yes, of course, but, more of that later.

October 23rd to November 5th 1942 had not been the Battle of Alamein.

It had been the Massacre at Alamein.

The use of the word 'massacre' implies unnecessary loss of life, and that is something this book will apply itself to presently.

In the meantime we will study what Rommel referred to as Montgomery's 'failure of pursuit'. It concerns Montgomery's slowness of reaction along the whole of the 1,000 mile seven month chase during which Rommel constantly remained one step ahead of the Allies. From the very beginning, to mention but one such example, General Briggs had urged that an armoured division with sufficient fuel and ammunition be ready to pounce (LRDG-like) and cut off Rommel's retreat but Montgomery had preferred to keep all his fuel and ammunition for his own plan of inch-by-inch advance. Rommel thus escaped at el Daba, at Fuka, and all the way to eventually meeting the Americans in west North Africa in May 1943. Even then he escaped to Italy.

Rommel thus escaped capture, so it was General von Thoma who was

151

brought before Montgomery. Shortly after this meeting Montgomery met the press and told them that he had boasted to von Thoma; **"I came to the desert in August to beat Rommel, in September I met Rommel, in October I defeated Rommel!"**

And in another statement he said, "I was told to go down to the desert and beat Rommel, and I did!"

"I", "I", "I". First person singular.

Veni, vidi, vici. I came, I saw, I conquered. If we are going to make classical allusions (as recorded by the Roman biographer Suetonius in 'The Twelve Caesars' circa 100 A.D.) let us remember Pyrrhus, King of Epirus, whose victory over the Romans at Asculum (279 B.C.) was so costly it was deemed that he could not afford too many victories of that kind. Was Montgomery's victory at Alamein a Pyrrhic victory? Many believe fervently that it was. He was quick to take full credit, therefore, if it was Pyrrhic then he must bear the blame.

Montgomery insisted that "I did it my way!", and no-one there argued with that claim!

At the early press conferences he made no mention of what he owed to the troops, and he made no mention of what Auchinleck and others had done.

Some in Cairo, and many in civilian life since, have said, 'Good old Montgomery!' not knowing the full story.

Others in Cairo, and many in civilian life since, have replied to Montgomery's claims and in particular his boast to von Thoma by using the Forces' most explosive military expletive of the day, "Bullshit!"

What do you think?

Could Alamein have been fought differently and with a much smaller loss of life? Of course it could.

Consider these two battles: ONE: 2nd Alamein Aug/Sept, and TWO: 3rd Alamein Oct/Nov 1942.

ONE: Montgomery can surely be taken to task for not following a defeated enemy after the Alam Halfa battle was clearly won by September 7th. Consider the significance of the date. September 9th was the original date Auchinleck had in mind to annihilate Rommel's forces, and, on September 7th the Axis Army was there for the taking.

MASSACRE AT ALAMEIN?

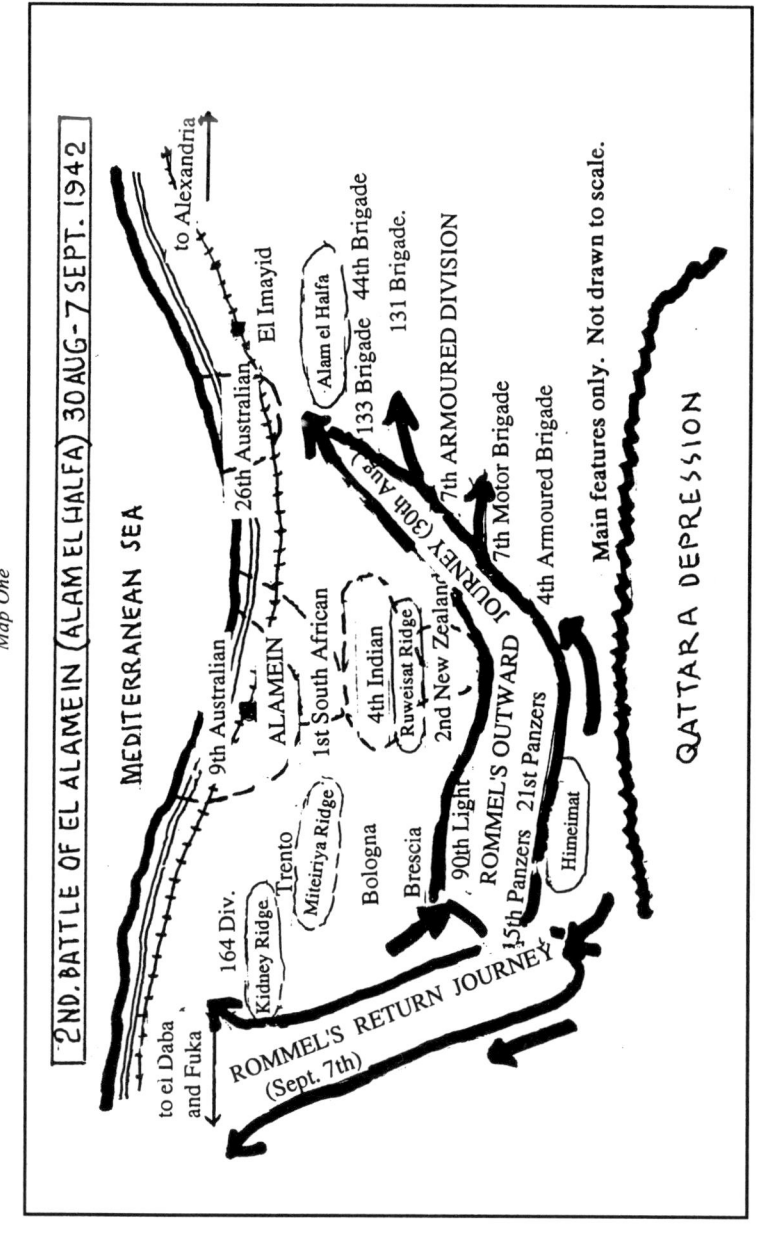

Map One

MASSACRE AT ALAMEIN?

Rommel had failed in the 1st Battle of Alamein (30th June) because for him it was a do-or-die bluff which he hoped would fool Auchinleck. Rommel needed speed, space and bluff but because he could only muster 55 tanks and his men had suffered five sleepless weeks of hard slog fighting their way into the Alamein Ambush he soon realised he was asking too much, gave in to Auchinleck's strength, and retired to a position west of the northern end of the Alamein Line. And now his second attempt had failed. (On August 30th Rommel wrote to his wife about this 'last Battle of Alamein'. '... *we have some very grave shortages. But I've taken the risk. If our blow succeeds, it might go some way towards deciding the whole course of the war. If it fails ...*' General Bayerlein reported that after writing this letter Rommel turned to Professor Dr. Horster and said, '...*either we reach the Suez Canal, or ...*' and he made a gesture of defeat).

And defeat is what he had suffered.

An orthodox pursuit by the Allies would have surrounded the exhausted Germans and Italians and Rommel would have had no alternative but to surrender. He was without fuel, tanks, his Italian comrades were less than half-hearted for a scrap, the RAF was bombing day and night, the Royal Navy was sinking Axis shipping, the LRDG and SAS patrols were cutting off land supplies along coastal road and blowing up their reserve supply dumps. It was happening as Auchinleck had planned. The aura of terror and lack of the ability to sleep restfully meant that Rommel's men feared the deadly night bombing of the RAF raids, and, in the morning on seeing their dead and the damage to transport and armour the RAF raids had caused, the Axis Army was in no shape to resist a rampant and victorious enemy. Even if Rommel had had enough fuel to retire to Fuka, RAF air photos showed that there were no defences at Fuka, or el Daba.

So, why? WHY? **WHY?** did Montgomery halt?

Rommel sent a firm report to Berlin, '*Our offensive no longer has any hope of success.*'

He then recorded his views, '... *the British had assembled powerful armoured forces between Alam el Halfa and Bab el Alamein and THEN REMAINED STATIONARY IN THEIR ASSEMBLY AREAS!* (Caps mine.

MASSACRE AT ALAMEIN?

B.L.). *The impression we gained of the new British Commander, General Montgomery, was that of a very cautious man.*'

Montgomery declared that he was content to '*proceed methodically with my own preparations for a big offensive later on.*'

To those on the spot and used to desert warfare, and those of us studying Air Survey maps, Montgomery's answer seems totally inadequate.

Montgomery restrained all those who showed a natural eagerness to follow up Rommel's retreat with the objective of extracting total surrender of the Axis forces. Rommel was down and out. The troops who chased him from Alam el Halfa back to his position west of the Alamein Line referred to it as 'the six day race', and then?, it was halted by Montgomery. Auchinleck, Gott, or even the lowest ranked Desert Rat would have followed up the Alam Halfa victory with an equally victorious pursuit. That is what had been planned!

Ah, but that would have been using Auchinleck's plan. No laurels in that for Montgomery. Montgomery wanted to win using HIS plan.

There are those who have suggested that Montgomery was like a spoilt child with a new bat and ball but will only let boys of his own choice play and then under his rules.

TWO. Montgomery let seven weeks pass.

Time and publicity would establish his name in the minds of people. Lovely excuse: "I am building up superior forces so that there is no chance of another failure!"

In those seven weeks Montgomery went from STRONG to VERY STRONG. **In those seven weeks Rommel went from DOWN AND OUT to FULLY OPERATIONAL!**

Who gained most by the delay?

Compare the map of the 2nd Battle of Alamein, 30th August to 7th September, 1942 with the map for the 3rd Battle of Alamein, 23rd October to 4th November.

We at the mapping section of the South African Survey Unit, like those at the Survey HQ (512 Survey Unit at nearby Tura Caves) and the RAF Intelligence Mapping Unit at GHQ Cairo had a unique opportunity of watching progress at Alamein during Montgomery's seven weeks of waiting.

MASSACRE AT ALAMEIN?

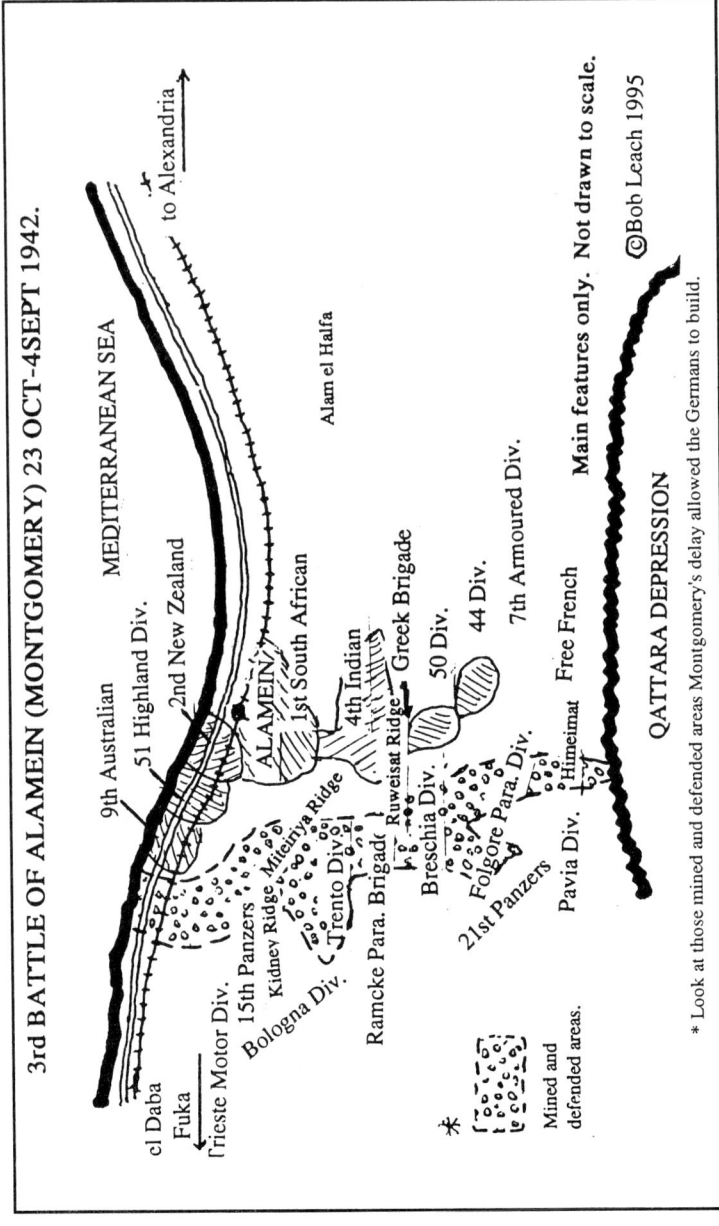

MASSACRE AT ALAMEIN?

Bear in mind that Rommel had no defences when he arrived at Alamein. Look at the 23rd October map and you will see that he had mined defences **all the way from the coast to the Qattara Depression!** That is what Montgomery's seven-week lull did. It revived Rommel's forces. He gained far far more than Montgomery did.

Look at those ferocious minefields Rommel's sappers had time to build.

Where, you might ask, did Rommel obtain all these thousands of mines if the Royal Navy was sinking Axis shipping and the RAF bombing supply dumps?

The answer is that the Italians had enormous supplies of mines. They loved to surround their camps with minefields. There was also local labour.

In 1941 the British, for example, issued contracts to Egyptian engineering companies to supply mines. The early ones were known as EPI, Egyptian Pattern Mark 1. However, it was soon discovered that a European specification for a mine had to modified for use in the desert. In the intense heat the gelignite sweated, creating nitroglycerin, and like the modern Magic Eye at Wimbledon Tennis Club they were likely to go off at unexpected times. The specification was improved and this supply added to the vast number of mines laid at Alamein.

Rommel also made use of local made mines and he gathered as many as he could from his dumps before the LRDG patrols blew them up. So, there was no shortage of mines.

Examine the map of the main features at Alamein on October 23rd 1942.

The front line troops at the northern end of the Alamein Line made a formidable army and it was quite right that their artillery barrage and advance should be on a massive scale, but, the front line troops in the southern section of the Line also made a formidable army **and they should have been used simultaneously with the northern army,** on the night of October 23/24th, not slogging on over the mines but in an orthodox sweeping movement to the rear of the enemy.

Consider not only the strength of this southern-end of Alamein Line army but also their special skills: the FRENCH. Where can one find better desert fighters than in the French Foreign Legion? and many of the Free

MASSACRE AT ALAMEIN?

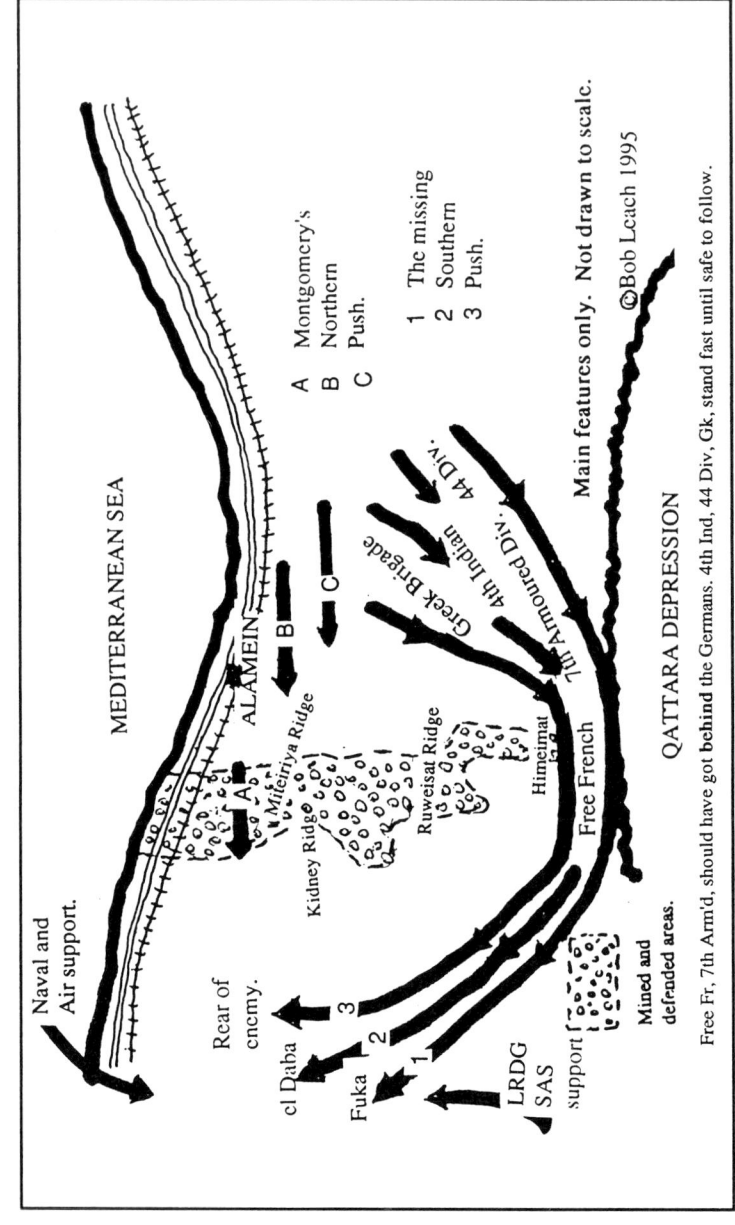

Map Three

French were experienced desert fighters; the 7th ARMOURED DIVISION, the famous Desert Rats, as desert wise as the LRDG itself; the 4th INDIAN DIVISION who had fought in every operation in the Western Desert since Wavell's first offensive in 1940; the new arrivals, 44th DIVISION who had acquitted themselves so well at the Alam el Halfa battle and deservedly earned their 'Desert Spurs'; and the GREEK BRIGADE, deadly keen fighters.

On the morning of October 24th this southern army should have been involved in a Rommel-Auchinleck-Gott style 'desert sweep', a flanking action directed at (1) the coastal air strip at Fuka, (2) el Daba, and (3) the rear of the enemy. See map illustrating this 'sweep'.

October 25th the LRDG and SAS patrols should have been co-operating with this southern sweep, and further support should have been coordinated with naval and air support **behind** the enemy positions at Alamein.

Bear in mind that a sweep of this nature **should have taken place on September 7th** when the Allies had Rommel on the run after Alam el Halfa.

However, Montgomery chose not to proceed with a chase after a beaten enemy and so the Allies were faced with this third Battle of Alamein beginning on October 23rd.

It should be the aim of every commander to achieve his objective with the least possible loss of life.

The South Africans were becoming alarmed at Montgomery's tactics, and especially angry at his refusal to discuss tactics or to listen to those with desert experience. The previous November, during the very heavy fighting in Auchinleck's push towards Benghazi, there had been an occasion when the 1st South African Brigade (Brigadier Dan Pienaar) became isolated at Bir el Gubi, 20 miles inland. The 5th South African Brigade (Brigadier Armstrong) was about 10 miles to the north, supported by the remnants of the 22 Armoured Brigade and the remnants of 7 Support Group. It made sense to gather these 'remnants' together and General Gott issued this order. It was important to close ranks because Rommel was using the classic desert manoeuvre of 'encircling' the enemy, that is, sweeping round and getting behind the enemy. Brigadier Pienaar realised that between him and Brigadier Armstrong were the combined forces of the Ariete Division, Panzer Regiments 5 and 8, and the formidable 15 Panzers. It would have been suicide to drive through a formation of that size. Pienaar made an alternative suggestion and **in order to achieve the objective with the least possible loss of life** General Gott allowed Pienaar to use common sense, circumnavigate the enemy forces, and join ranks with 5 South African Brigade with minimum loss of life.

Montgomery seemed to be pathetically unable to present His Plan for scrutiny or discussion by his senior officers.

Not only were the South Africans becoming alarmed at Montgomery's profligate use of human life but so was the Australian High Command and a complaint was issued on behalf of the Australian Forces in the desert. The dedication to battle by the Empire troops was tremendous, but dedication is something that must not be abused or taken advantage of.

The song, *There'll always be an England* has a middle section and the words are, *The Empire too, We can depend on you!* and my Goodness, that dependence on Empire troops had been absolutely essential to both Wavell and Auchinleck. Nevertheless, there are limits and if at times the Empire Troops were almost too brave for their own good it was up to their High Commands to see that this bravery and loyalty was not abused. They did not like being treated as cannon fodder, that is, troops sent blindly into battle on the order of one Haig-like dictatorial man. Let their own senior officers have a say in what was being planned.

The first words of criticism in late 1942 which I personally heard came from the South Africans and I could see their point of view.

Was human life being carelessly thrown away?

Over a period of months (versus Italy) Wavell lost 500 killed.

Over a period of months (versus Germany) Auchinleck lost 2,900 killed.

Over a period of days at Alamein (Aug 30–Sept 7) using barrage and southern sweep desert tactics 1,630 Allied troops were killed. (General Alexander's official list).

This battle was as fiercely fought as the final battle on October 23rd.

Over a similar period of days under the Montgomery Plan of using only

a northern barrage and congested northern push forward (October 23-
November 4th) with no southern sweep the Allied loss of life at Alamein
was 7,942 (Commonwealth War Graves register of cemetries figures).

**Montgomery's Plan lost at least six men killed to every one by either
Auchinleck or Rommel!**

*A particularly chilling statistic is that 6,904 British lives were lost in
Japan's infamous Death Railway through Burma,* **1,038 LESS than
Montgomery threw away at Alamein!**

I have visited the Alamein Cemetery. All those lonely gravestones. Too
many. Too many men died. Done the Montgomery way it was a massacre.

What do you think?

Fifty years after the war secret papers were released and historian David
Saul's book, *Mutiny at Salerno,* makes reference to an occasion at Salerno
in 1943 when men, mostly from the 50th (Tyne Tees) and 51st (Highland)
Division . . . **members of the Eighth Army of desert fame** . . . refused to
fight at the bridgehead established at Salerno. The bridgehead was facing
collapse and these men had been told by their camp commandant that they
were being returned to their unit. The men were either suffering from
wounds or from dysentry and were in no condition to fight a desperate
battle. They had been told a deliberate lie. A review of David Saul's book
inspired the startling headline: PARDON DEMANDED FOR
MONTGOMERY 'MUTINEERS' (21st September 1995). Sir Ludovic
Kennedy said that the mutiny was a spontaneous reaction from men 'who
felt they had been messed about enough'. It is true that this lie to the men
was not perpetrated by Montgomery but Sir Ronald Adam, the Adjutant-
General wrote to Montgomery saying that the arrest of the men *was one
of the worst things we have ever done.* Nevertheless, the trial went ahead.
David Saul called it a 'charade of a trial'.

Three men were given a death sentence (firing squad), later commuted,
and the rest were given prison terms of between 5 and 10 years. They were
stripped of their campaign medals (one man had the Military Medal),
branded as mutineers, suffered ill-health and nervous breakdowns, and
after the war a psychiatrist's report cleared them of cowardice and, *more
than fifty years after the trial Montgomery could have stopped* David Saul
sent a letter to Michael Portillo, the Defence Secretary, pleading that 'only

MASSACRE AT ALAMEIN?

by granting a free pardon can a handful of the surviving mutineers and the families be released from the torment which has gripped them since 1943'.

A tragic and insensitive ending for men who had fought their hearts out chasing the Germans from Alamein to Tripoli . . . one thousand bloodstained miles of sand.

CHAPTER TWELVE

Let Us Now Praise Famous Men

It is not the purpose of this book to be iconoclastic. The purpose can be understood quite clearly and dispassionately by examining the facts and posing the question: *Were Generals Wavell and Auchinleck treated unjustly and was Montgomery over-rated during the desert wars of 1940/41, 1941/42, and 1942/43?*

The first title I thought of for the book was UNJUST DESERTS, but although Wavell and Auchinleck may not have received their 'just deserts' the title suggests that it is 'the desert' which has been unjust, whereas I am making a case to prove that it is 'history' which has been unjust.

If the reader can now appreciate what desert commanders other than Montgomery did to prepare for the Victory at Alamein then I will feel that my book has achieved its purpose.

Lawrence of Arabia states that those who live in the desert emerge a little wiser and a little more generous in manner. That Christmas in 1942, when Montgomery knew that he was a national hero, he appreciated what David Stirling had done and he sent to the men in the Desert Patrol with Stirling a bottle of whisky each and 200 (English!) cigarettes.

The stories we read of Montgomery telling troops to break ranks and sit on the ground while he stands and talks to them I can accept as being excellent tactics and good leadership. But that was after Alamein, and I do not sit in judgement during that latter period. I have written about Montgomery before Alamein, and I have done so to bring credit where credit is due, to Wavell, Auchinleck, Gott, Rommel, von Thoma, Graziani, Jock Campbell, Alexander, Ritchie, Stirling, Freyberg, Popski, Derek Rawnsley, and dozens of others who were 'desert warriors' and became part of those two unique never-to-be-repeated corps, THE DESERT RATS and THE AFRIKA KORPS. The Desert Storm in Iraq against Sadam Hussein fifty years after Alamein proves that the conditions in the 1940–42 desert wars will never return. Advanced weaponry will see to that.

When the war in North Africa was all over, on May 13 1943, Rommel described the desert battles as *a war without hate.* It had been fought bitterly, but with honour and an almost 'olde world' chivalry.

The desert wars, so unique and special, linger in the memory like noble dreams. More than half a century has passed and no war since 1942 has been able to anywhere near equal the 'sporting flavour' of the 1940–1942 wars in the hot sands of Egypt. It is unlikely that we will ever again see such a 'war without hate', as Rommel called it.

I completed the first draft of this book in July 1995 and it so happened that this coincided with an end-of-term dinner with my wife's choir. The young lady (with her husband) sitting opposite to me asked quite casually, in the listless way strangers sometimes open a conversation, what book I was working on and I replied that I had just completed a non-fiction work on the desert wars. Her eyes lit up. Usually when an author mentions a book he/she is working on other eyes suddenly grow wary and distant!

"Ah, Rommel, he saved my father's life. The Germans over-ran the British camp and my father tore the maps from the wall. A German officer told my father he would be shot for that. Then Rommel himself came in and said that his men would have done just the same as my father and that he was not to be shot but treated as an ordinary prisoner of war."

"What was your father's name? Is he still alive?" I asked.

"His name was Ken Wakefield. He died in 1986."

I am sure we were each thinking the same thing. Her father had lived for a further 44 years after capture thanks to Rommel's humanity and, but for that, she (Audrey, nee Wakefield) would never have been born.

With the best will in the world I cannot equate a man like Montgomery with the desert commanders I served under during 1940–1942.

MASSACRE AT ALAMEIN?

It was the nearest that war could ever get to 'Sport'.

Sir Henry John Newbolt, the English poet who died in 1938, summed up the sporting spirit of that age:

There's a breathless hush in the close tonight . . .
Ten to make and the match to win . . .

But his captain's band on his shoulder smote,
Play up! Play up! and play the game!
                          (Vitai Lampada)

Rudyard Kipling in a poem on Boxing *(from his Verses on Games.)* writes of:

. . . blown by many overthrows,
Half blind with shame, half choked with dirt,
Man cannot tell, but Allah knows,
How much the other side was hurt!

General Wavell includes this in his collection of poems entitled *Other Men's Flowers* and he adds a note: 'The last two lines illustrate my favourite military maxim, that when things are going badly in battle the best tonic is to take one's mind off one's own troubles by considering what a rotten time one's opponent must be having.' A.P.W.

Lawrence of Arabia is but one of many who believe that the desert not only induces such benefits as wisdom and tolerance but also a greater love of the arts: painting, poetry, music. A recent publication *The Voice of War,* published by Michael Joseph in 1995, is a collection of poems and those by 'desert poets' form an important part of the collection. General Wavell concludes his own collection by modestly confessing that he was urged to include a sonnet he had written in 1943, *Sonnet for the Madonna of the Cherries,* which concludes:

Your red-gold hair, your slowly smiling face,
For pride in your dear son, your King of Kings,

MASSACRE AT ALAMEIN?

Fruits of the kindly earth, and truth and grace,
Colour and light, and all warm lovely things . . .
For all that loveliness, that warmth, that light,
Blessed Madonna, I go back to fight.

I close with my own photograph of the desert memorial at Tobruk for the dead taken while I was with Derek Rawnsley's LRI Desert Patrol, 1941/42.

At the going down of the sun
And in the morning
We will remember them.

At The Going Down of the Sun

CODA

The 512 Royal Engineers Survey Company remained in Egypt long after the Desert Forces left Africa. Egypt, with its long history of being the place where East meets West, was ideal for world-wide target map-making when the war spread northwest into Europe and southeast into India, Asia, China and Japan.

Bob Leach's three years in Egypt continued for another two and during this period (1943/44) he helped with the music and sport of his company. A testimonial from his then commanding officer is illustrative of this period during which the pros and cons of the desert wars were discussed both in military terms and civilian. Elsewhere in the world the progress of the war was concentrated on where the action was taking place. To the world ALAMEIN was an important victory, forever referred to as **the turning point of the war.**

No need to analyse it. A victory is a victory. That is how 'the world' saw it.

Who was the victor at Alamein . . . ? "Oh, yes, that chap Montgomery. Waited until he had superior forces, didn't he?" It is so easy to think like that.

But to most who were there under Wavell, Auchinleck and Gott . . . it seems so unfair that the credit should go so blindly where it has, to Montgomery.

167

MASSACRE AT ALAMEIN?

Tel: TUDOR 6627

26 Beech Drive,
East Finchley. London
N2.
31.3.'47

Robert C Leach.

I have known Robert Leach for many years. He served in the Middle East under my command during the war during which time among his many other interests he was responsible for the musical activities of a company of some 500 men. He was also lagely responsible for the organisation of their sport and recreation.

He is a man of wide musical knowledge, an instrumentalist and a composer and I cannot speak too highly of his enthusiasm for all types of musical expression.

He is a fine athlete and his organising and administrative abilities have been proved beyond question.

As a man I know from personal experience that he is most trustworthy and intensely loyal to those in authority. Socially he is a most pleasant companion and I have considered myself fortunate to count him as one of my friends.

W.K Sykes. Late Lt.-Col. R.E

MASSACRE AT ALAMEIN? by Bob Leach
can be ordered from any bookshop
(Quote ISBN 1 899955 09 7)

or from SQUARE ONE PUBLICATIONS,
The Tudor House, 16 Church Street,
Upton-upon-Severn, Worcs WR8 0HT

UK Price £4.99 . . . plus £1.85 pst/pkg
